The Financial Times
Guide to Financial
Spread Betting

PEARSON

At Pearson, we believe in learning – all kinds of learning for all kinds of people. Whether it's at home, in the classroom or in the workplace, learning is the key to improving our life chances.

That's why we're working with leading authors to bring you the latest thinking and the best practices, so you can get better at the things that are important to you. You can learn on the page or on the move, and with content that's always crafted to help you understand quickly and apply what you've learned.

If you want to upgrade your personal skills or accelerate your career, become a more effective leader or more powerful communicator, discover new opportunities or simply find more inspiration, we can help you make progress in your work and life.

Pearson is the world's leading learning company. Our portfolio includes the Financial Times, Penguin, Dorling Kindersley, and our educational business, Pearson International.

Every day our work helps learning flourish, and wherever learning flourishes, so do people.

To learn more please visit us at: www.pearson.com/uk

The Financial Times Guide to Spread Betting

Stuart Fieldhouse

PEARSON

Harlow, England • London • New York • Boston • San Francisco • Toronto • Sydney • Auckland • Singapore • Hong Kong
Tokyo • Seoul • Taipei • New Delhi • Cape Town • São Paulo • Mexico City • Madrid • Amsterdam • Munich • Paris • Milan

PEARSON EDUCATION LIMITED

Edinburgh Gate
Harlow CM20 2JE
Tel: 144 (0)1279 623623
Fax: 144 (0)1279 431059
Website: www.pearson.com/uk

First published in Great Britain in 2012

ISBN: 978–0–273–75046–8

British Library Cataloguing-in-Publication Data
A catalogue record for this book is available from the British Library

Library of Congress Cataloging-in-Publication Data
Fieldhouse, Stuart.
  The Financial times guide to spread betting / Stuart Fieldhouse.
    p. cm.
  Includes indexes.
  ISBN 978-0-273-75046-8 (pbk.)
  1. Electronic trading of securities--Great Britain. 2. Spread betting--Great Britain. 3. Speculation--Great Britain. 4. Investments--Great Britain. I. Financial times (London, England) II. Title.
  HG4515.95.F54 2012
  332.63'2280941--dc23
                          2011043050

10 9 8 7 6 5 4 3 2 1
15 14 13 12 11

Typeset in 9/13pt ITC Stone Serif Std by 3
Printed by Ashford Colour Press Ltd., Gosport

To Vanja, Sebastian and Maya. For all their love and patience.

Contents

Author's acknowledgements

A number of people have contributed their time and expertise in helping me to write this book, all of it invaluable. In particular, I'd like to thank Vanya Dragomanovich, commodities editor at FTSE Global Markets, for her help with the commodities chapter, Michael van Dulken at Accendo Markets, who provided much help and advice on the technical analysis section, and Bill McIntosh, editor of *The Hedgefund Journal*, who cast his expert eye over the shares and indexes chapter. Grant Fuller of Axicorda placed his considerable knowledge of futures markets and risk management at my disposal. Thanks must also go to Mariya Rysin at CMC Markets, Michael Morton at The Armchair Trader, and Shah Zaman at Accendo Markets, all of whom have given freely of their time and knowledge in helping this book reach fruition. Finally, thanks to Ashraf Laidi for all his invaluable insights into forex and rates markets over the last few years. Thank you all for being so generous.

Publisher's acknowledgements

We are grateful to the following for permission to reproduce copyright material:

Figures

Figure 3.3 adapted from www.IT-finance.com, IT-Finance.com; Figure 3.5 adapted from www.livecharts.co.uk, LiveCharts.co.uk; Figures 4.1, 4.2 Reproduced with permission of Yahoo! Inc. ©2011 Yahoo! Inc. YAHOO! and the YAHOO! logo are registered trademarks of Yahoo! Inc.; Figures 6.1, 6.2, 8.2, 8.3, 8.6, 8.8 from Alpha Terminal, www.alphaterminal.co.uk; Figure 6.3 from www.ProRealTime.com, IT-Finance.com; Figures 6.1, 6.2, 8.2, 8.3, 8.6, 8.8 from www.alphaterminal.co.uk, Alpha Terminal; Figure 8.7 provided by Action Forex (http://www.actionforex.com).

In some instances we have been unable to trace the owners of copyright material, and we would appreicate any information that would enable us to do so.

Introduction: What is financial spread betting?

Financial spread betting is the fastest growing form of online trading in the UK today. The increasing use of the internet for trading activities, coupled with an interest on the part of the public in trading other financial markets outside physical share markets, has led to this spectacular growth. Financial spread betting has the additional attraction of being tax free, with no capital gains tax or stamp duty levied on transactions.

Advertising by the companies that offer spread betting is ubiquitous, on railway station billboards, in business newspapers and even on television. But for someone who is not familiar with spread betting, it can look dauntingly complex from the outside.

This book sets out to be a primer for the beginner interested in the world of spread betting; there is information within that can guide you through the early stages of your spread betting career, as well as chapters that will become of more interest once you have placed your first few trades.

Before you hit that 'buy' button and immerse yourself in the world of online financial markets that spread betting offers you access to, it is vitally important that you make sure you know what you're doing.

Every day, hundreds of people open and fund an online financial spread betting account, often lured by special offers or the attractive prospect of being able to pocket any profits without paying tax. Perhaps it is the glamour of trading fast-moving financial markets that causes individuals to stake thousands of pounds on trades that can lose them that stake – and more – in a matter of minutes.

Yet as with many things in life, online trading can be more rewarding if you do a little homework, spend some time informing yourself about the choices that you are being presented with and educate yourself about some of the risks you face as a trader. There are, after all, many lower risk ways to make money: that's what financial advisers and the multi-billion pound fund management industry is there for. But if you are taken with the idea of trading, and potentially generating some extra income for yourself (or even making a living from this eventually), then it is critically important that you only place your first live trade once you are completely sure of the risks you are taking on.

To many who have not placed a trade online, financial spread betting probably seems like an esoteric, inaccessible and high risk area of investment. Parallels are sometimes drawn with gambling, especially sports spread betting. To all intents and purposes, spread betting *is* gambling, in that you are betting on price movements and not paying tax on your winnings. The UK tax authorities treat it as gambling for this very reason. The prices you trade on are not the market prices: they are very similar, and it takes skill to make money from this consistently, but you are not trading the market itself.

While spread betting companies are regulated as investment firms by the Financial Services Authority (FSA), a spread betting account is an opportunity to gamble on prices of financial markets. Spread betting is not investing.

Financial spread betting will also feel like gambling if you don't know what you're doing and simply open an account and start trading, which is what many new to this game do every month. Individuals with an addictive personality, or those who may suspect they could develop a gambling addiction given half a chance, would do well to stay out of spread betting.

All trading is, after all, a form of gambling. Like gambling – including betting on horses – it pays to get familiar with the market you want to trade. Taking a blind punt may work once or twice, but eventually you will lose. Later in this book we will go further into the topic of gathering information and getting a feel for financial markets. When starting out, it may all seem very confusing – you may not feel completely sure of the difference between stocks and bond markets even – but if you read this book, cover to cover, I hope you will come away from the experience with a much better idea of how to trade, which markets you want to trade, and the kind of strategy that will suit you, your lifestyle and your disposition as a human being.

Everybody is different, and very few traders are the same either. Financial spread betting may not be for everyone, but right now it represents one of the most cost-effective ways of accessing financial markets that it would be difficult – and expensive – to access in other ways.

The tax free approach to trading

In the UK and Ireland, financial spread betting is a tax free way to trade a broad range of financial markets online. Money made this way is not subject to capital gains tax or stamp duty. From a taxation perspective, spread betting is regarded as gambling, in that gambling proceeds are not taxed, and it is important to realise that in some ways spread betting can be more risky than betting on horses: you can lose more money than you put down. But spread betting is the most tax efficient way to access the highly liquid world of futures trading, including commodities, currencies and interest rate markets.

Spread betting grew out of futures trading, and in some ways spread bets can still resemble futures. Futures markets were historically closed to the retail investor; they were the demesne of big banks and fund managers, and this was due to the large minimum trade sizes required to buy and sell futures and options contracts. Now, spread betting allows you to potentially profit from some of the price action of the futures market, but for considerably less money up front.

Spread betting also gives private individuals an unprecedented opportunity to trade global markets without many of the 'drag' costs and currency risks associated with buying and selling physical assets like shares and property. Indeed, in many respects, the opportunity gap between professional money managers and the retail investor is narrower than ever before. The range of markets, the technology, the pricing information, all of this was once only the preserve of professionals. Now it is being delivered to private individuals for a fraction of the cost.

The prime brokers, the big banks which provide professional investors with access to financial markets, also provide spread betting companies with the same prices they give to the pros. I will go into more detail later about the hidden fees involved in trading, but even so, spread betting represents an opportunity for knowledgeable individuals to watch prices in real time – not the 15-minute delayed prices you see on a news website – get up-to-the-second intelligence on the markets, and execute trades on currency, share and commodity prices instantaneously.

An online trading revolution

The introduction of online spread betting in the mid-1990s has really revolutionised the way we, as private individuals, can access financial markets.

The trading industry is innovating all the time: there are more sources of information, more products designed for the trading customer appearing every week. It can be bewildering at times. But it shouldn't be.

This book sets out to inform the complete beginner about not only spread betting, but also the new markets to which spread betting can offer access. Many newcomers to spread betting will have bought and sold shares in the physical market, or have invested in a few funds or investment trusts. Spread betting requires an awareness of the dynamics driving the futures markets that lie behind the prices you will see on your trading screen, and you will need to be aware of the additional risks and opportunities these markets offer, and whether they are something that appeals to you personally.

This book addresses the practicalities of spread betting in this Introduction and Chapter 1. I would also recommend that any novice should read the chapter on risk management before they even think of opening a spread betting account. This book also offers information on the spread betting firms themselves, and what sorts of services they can offer. In the Appendix you will find more information on some of the leading companies.

Spread betting offers the newcomer access to prices of the main share markets, individual stocks and a whole gamut of brand new asset classes which are increasingly making headline news these days. This includes commodities, currencies and bonds, not to mention interest rates. Each has its own chapter as well as information on how to trade these markets using a spread betting account, and what to look out for.

Finally, we end with the topic of technical analysis, resources and how to develop your own unique trading style. While not essential, these chapters will help you to understand much of what you see and hear about in the world of spread betting and trading in general, and may serve to open up new avenues for the more seasoned spread bettor as well.

If you've read as far as this, you are likely to be someone who is determined to find out more about financial spread betting, and the opportunities and rewards it can offer. Read on, and we'll address some of the basics. I would not recommend placing a trade after reading this Introduction, but it will provide you with enough information to be able to hold your own on the subject at a cocktail party! By the time you have perused this book in its entirety, however, you should have a good understanding of the spread betting industry, how it all works and what to look out for.

How not to lose your shirt ...

From the outset, this book assumes that you are not a financial professional, that you do not work in the City of London, and that you may not even have traded shares online before. Indeed, there is no real need to have had prior experience of trading financial markets in order to open a spread betting account and get started. Spread betting is not something reserved for City traders who want to punt the markets after hours: most of the professional traders I've met would rather do anything but continue trading in their spare time!

What has impressed me about spread betting's existing client base in the UK is its sheer diversity: people from all walks of life and backgrounds are already active traders. I have met retired people who spread bet, and traders who are university students in their early twenties. More than one housewife is supplementing their monthly income by trading in between school drop off and pick up. Others get home from work and trade currency markets rather than watch television. For some it is a hobby, for others a lifestyle. With the introduction of mobile technology, it is now possible to trade wherever you can find an internet connection. Whether it is a good thing to be almost continually connected to the markets is debatable, but the opportunity is now there for those who want it.

It is, however, important that you understand the risks involved in spread betting, that you know exactly what it is you are trading, and that you also have a fair idea of what the company providing you with your account is allowed to do, and what it is not allowed to do. There is no point complaining if the firm you trade with is acting within the limits of the regulations laid down by the Financial Services Authority.

However, it is extremely important that you fully understand the risks involved in spread betting, particularly the use of leverage. This is not something that spread betting companies spend a lot of time educating their customers about, and many new traders find out about trading on leverage the hard way. What it boils down to is this: you can lose more money on a trade than you risk at first.

Financial spread betting allows you to trade on margin. This means you only need to put down a fraction of the total value of the trade (called 'the margin'), but you can pocket the whole profit. For example, if a share is quoted to you as having 10 per cent margin, and the price of the share is £100, you only need to put down £10. If the share goes up to £120, you still get to keep that £20 profit, and you keep your £10 risk capital too. You've tripled your money.

This sounds great in practice, and is often blandished around as one of the great attractions of financial spread betting, but think for a moment about the amount of risk you are taking on.

If you bought a share in the physical market – and when I refer to the physical market in this book, I mean a market where you are actually buying a physical asset, be it a share, or a barrel of oil or even a house, something you can own or use – you are buying a share in a company. You own a piece of that company. If the price goes down, and you sell that share, it is still worth something to other people. You may lose some of your money on that investment, but you can usually find someone else to buy it off you in the market, or at least your stockbroker can. In the most extreme case, you could lose all your money if the company goes bankrupt. That is the worst that can happen to you with physical share trading.

With financial spread betting, your trade is not in the physical market. It is based on prices of physical assets in the most part (but not always – and we will look at some of these interesting, but exceptional, markets later). Your trade is really just a contract between you and your spread betting company. You don't own anything. Your spread betting company is acting, in many respects, as a bookie.

Like gambling, a spread bet can go badly awry. Take the above example of that £100 spread bet on a share price. I'm trading at 10 per cent margin, and I stake £10. But this time the price of the share drops to £90. I've now lost my £10, and I get what is called a 'margin call' from my broker, a request to fund that trade with more real money, otherwise my trade will be closed.

I'm still feeling good about this trade, so I finance it to the tune of a further £10. But the price drops again, and now I'm £20 out of pocket. I don't have an asset I can sell to someone else. I have simply lost my initial risk capital, and then managed to double that loss. And that price can keep on going south, and drag me down with it, if I let it.

Bear in mind financial markets can move quickly, and by the time you get that margin call, you could have lost much more than your £10 initial deposit. If you are sitting on a big cash position in your trading account, it is possible that your broker might let the trade run without a friendly phone call, and by the time you next look at your screen, you could be £30 or £40 out of pocket. This may not seem like a lot of money, but some traders, once they become more confident, will be putting a zero, or two zeroes on the end of that. Spread betting can be a big money game, but you don't want to have to dip into the equity in your house to finance it. Trade using cash you can afford to lose, not with your pension money, emergency savings or any money that is needed for something else.

Some readers out there will be looking at that leveraged trading scenario and wondering: where is the rest of the money coming from? It is effectively a loan from your spread betting company. Start thinking of it like that, and you will take your first big step on the road to effective risk management. If you are trading on 10 per cent margin, someone else is loaning you 90 per cent of the value of the trade. That's very nice of them, but don't worry too much about sending them a bottle of whisky at Christmas, because they will get their pound of flesh off you in other ways (and we'll also look at that later on in this book).

You will see some markets quoted at 1 per cent margin: this means your broker, your counterparty, is lending you 99 per cent of the trade. Sometimes this is needed, particularly in markets where the change in price is measured by tiny increments, but in other situations it is not, and this is where new traders can get into difficulties. On such occasions it is time to 'dial down on the risk' as they say in the money management industry. Just because someone is offering to lend you the money to trade with, doesn't mean that you should take it.

I hope that by this stage I've not scared you off the idea of financial spread betting completely. But this is an important issue, and it is why I decided to devote an entire chapter to risk management later on in this book. Professional money managers are obsessed about risk management these days, and there is no reason why private money managers shouldn't be either.

1

How to spread bet

When opening a spread betting account for the first time, you will be faced with a bewildering array of new markets and products to trade. Some spread betting companies offer their customers literally thousands of different prices to choose from, including indexes, currencies, shares, commodities, bonds, interest rates, even volatility. Seeing it all glinting in greens and reds on your screen may make you want to run away, or it may have the opposite effect, letting you feel suddenly connected to the multi-trillion dollar world of global financial markets. Read this book through, however, and it will all start to make more sense.

First, let's look a bit more closely at how a spread bet works. To begin with, once you have opened a spread betting account, and funded it with real money (the initial deposit required will vary according to the provider you are using), you will no doubt want to start trading right away. Many companies will offer you the capability to do some trading with no money at all using a demonstration or 'demo' account, and I would encourage you to do this for a while, in order to get comfortable not only with the processes involved, but also with the way the platform you are using to trade on works. You can do this before opening a live account. Some companies will offer you only a limited number of markets to trade on, or will only let you have access for a limited period of time – two weeks, for example.

One big difference with demo accounts, however – you will never have any problems with liquidity. Your buy and sell trades will always be met because, at the end of the day, this is just a sophisticated computer game until you put some real money in. Nobody at the other end is having to hedge any market exposure. This can create the illusion that you will always be able to buy and sell at the price you want, but in live trading conditions, this will not always be possible.

Spread betting markets

There are now many different trading platforms out there, some better than others, and most spread betting companies have spent a lot of money in the development of their own proprietary trading platforms.

All spread bets will be quoted using two prices, not one. This is called the bid/offer spread, and is the same as buying or selling foreign currency across the counter at a bank or post office. There is one price to buy, and one price to sell, and the buy price is always higher than the sell price. The difference in the prices is called the spread. In financial spread betting, this is a major source of competition between the various brokers, as they seek to attract customers by offering narrower and narrower spreads. You will frequently see the most popular markets will have very small spreads, with only a few points' difference. Some markets now have only a single point between the two prices, making them very cheap indeed to trade. The hope, of course, is that traders will be tempted to trade other markets as well, where the spread is a lot wider.

Each market will also have a margin rate, as previously described. This represents the amount of money you will need to post up front when you open the trade. It will vary between 1 per cent, all the way up to 50 per cent in some extreme cases (see Table 1.1 for some examples of margins quoted by a typical spread betting company). These rates were correct at the time of writing, but they can change quickly as a result of market conditions. Consequently, it is worth checking with companies, shopping around or visiting independent websites like The Armchair Trader (www.thearmchairtrader.com).

Now you have to decide how much money you want to risk. With spread betting, this involves staking an amount of money per point the price moves. A typical example would be £1/point on the FTSE 100 index, but it could just as easily be the pound against the dollar, or the spot gold price.

If the FTSE 100 goes up, you're making money to the tune of how many points it has risen. Bear in mind, however, that there is still that ugly spread to get across before you are really making money, as you only have a solid profit once you're past the sell price quoted by your broker. Still, with a six point spread, for example, the index would only need to climb six points before you're across that gap.

Profits – and losses – in spread betting are measured in points. The more money you attach to each point, the bigger your risk and the larger your potential profits or losses. If the FTSE closed up 25 points today, and my bet was staked at £1 per point, I'd make £25 (minus the spread, of course). If I staked £3 per point instead, I'd make £75.

Once you decide to sell your position, you hit the sell button, and you've closed your trade. If you've made a profit, you've done it tax free, as spread betting profits are not taxed in the UK.

Shorting the market

One of the key advantages that spread betting enjoys over conventional share trading is the ability to short assets. By this I mean making money

Table 1.1: Margins on typical spread betting markets, 2011

UK 100	1%
US 30	1%
Euro 50	1%
Japan 225	1%
Hong Kong 43	1%
Vodafone	3%
Apple Inc.	5%
Swiss Life	8%
GBP/USD	1%
EUR/USD	1%
USD/JPY	1%
EUR/CHF	1%
Gold	1%
Silver	1%
Soybean	3%
Sugar	3%
UK 10yr Gilt	1%

Note: The above is a list of typical minimum margins you might encounter from a spread betting company. These are subject to change, particularly if interbank lending deteriorates. As you can see, most of the major spread betting contracts have very low margin rates. The main area of variation is with shares. Even a FTSE 100 stock like Vodafone will have a 3 per cent margin. Rates will vary between companies, although it is unlikely to be less than 1 per cent.

from falling prices. Just because the market falls out of bed doesn't mean you have to lose money. It means that you, as a trader, can make money out of fear as well as greed.

To 'go short' or 'short' a market you are essentially taking a position that will allow you to make money as the market falls. Instead of using the buy or bid order that your broker quotes you, you use the higher of the two prices, the sell or offer order. This means you will only profit if the price goes down, and you will lose money if the price goes up. Think of it as a trade in reverse, an inverse market scenario. It allows you to actually bet against a share price, or a commodity or an index. If you think it is going to fall, there's no reason not to short it.

The spread still applies, of course. If you wanted to liquidate this position, you would simply close it using the bid price rather than the offer price.

The risk with shorting is that while a price has a finite distance to travel to zero, it has scope for potentially infinite upside. You need to be especially careful when shorting individual shares, as share prices have a tendency to 'gap' up suddenly: a losing position created here, when you end up on the wrong side of a short trade, can run up a substantial loss.

In professional money management circles, good short side specialists are actually fairly rare. This is because many professional asset managers find it hard to actively short markets on an ongoing basis. However, if you are someone who can see where things are going to go wrong, or can sniff out over-priced assets (like the entire UK construction sector in early 2008 for example), you can make money on a regular basis off your short book.

Shorting also allows you to hedge your long positions, including perhaps share positions you hold outside your spread betting account. It can help you to minimise damage to your shares, for example by taking a short position on the FTSE 250 index. If your shares lose value in a sudden market down-turn, your spread bet will make you money and vice versa. In most cases, investors will use their hedge position to minimise damage to their portfolio – i.e. gains will replace some, but not all of the losses from the long side.

Finally, shorting also allows you to reverse your position in the market as sentiment changes, but here you need to time your exit from a long trade correctly, and then your re-entry as the market falls.

But what to trade?

Many people open trading accounts and start trading an index-based bet like the FTSE 100 or the S&P 500. Indeed, they are often encouraged to do so by spread betting companies on the basis that the FTSE is an easy-to-understand market for the beginner. But there are many more interesting markets available to trade on spread betting platforms, yet most traders never venture anywhere near them.

This book looks at the major financial markets to which spread betting gives you access. It provides enough information for you to start trading them. If a particular area of trading grabs you, then there is nothing wrong with jumping ahead to read about that. However, it is also critical that you make sure you understand the chapters on risk management and on finding the right broker for your purposes.

I have read many complaints from traders who have lost thousands of pounds spread betting, frequently blaming the company they trade with. More often than not, however, their losses occur because they have not understood the risks they are taking on board, or have not fully read and comprehended the terms and conditions they have signed up to when opening their account. I would urge anyone thinking of opening a spread betting account to read these chapters before making a live trade.

Finding the right company to trade with

Many experienced traders have more than one spread betting account. There are a number of good reasons for doing this, and if you can afford it, it can be worth doing. Spread betting companies come in all shapes and sizes: most will offer the same core range of markets, but beyond that there are many ways to differentiate them. Before opening an account, it is worth shopping around using the criteria that are important for you.

More and more spread betting companies are springing up all the time, and the competition for new accounts is getting fiercer. In addition, some of the major spread betting companies allow their trading platforms to be white-labelled by partners, including banks, stock brokers and independent financial advisers. This means an increasing number of people in the UK are being offered the chance to spread bet. Most of the time, all these trades are being channelled through the same handful of broker firms.

However, the increasing number of spread betting companies is still good news for you, the private trader, because it means you are able to shop around for the best trading account for your purposes. Judge firms by the criteria that are important to you as a trader: do not open an account simply because there is a special offer on, or a company is offering you £100 of its own money to open an account. It is worth doing some background research on companies on the internet, or checking out independent websites like The Armchair Trader, which have plenty of information on what exactly the various companies are offering, allowing you to weigh them against each other.

Spread betting companies are highly profitable entities. They make their money primarily on the spreads they offer on markets, but they also profit in other ways. Unlike investing in funds or physical shares, some of the costs associated with financial spread betting are not immediately obvious, and will differ from company to company. When trading it is useful to be aware of how your spread betting provider – your counterparty – is making money as well. Many complaints from new traders originate because they feel they are somehow being 'tricked' or 'short changed' by a firm. Often this boils down to the terms and conditions of the account that has been opened, or the specific trading instrument that is being used.

Take that £100 offer to open an account which I mentioned earlier. Where's the catch there? You can be sure there will be one entrenched in the terms and conditions. Take everything you are offered with a pinch of salt: ultimately, trading boils down to the price you are offered and can trade at. Everything else is just window dressing.

Once you have a firm you are happy using, I suggest you stick with them, and then open a second account to allow objective analysis of the service you are getting from your first spread betting shop. This is especially the case with prices and execution, allowing you to compare and contrast the service you are getting. And ultimately, price is a service in this game. As a trader you are relying on your broker to be able to find you the best price in the market.

What's in a price?

Although you may see a price quoted for a futures contract or share on an exchange, this will not necessarily be the price you see on your trading screen, or the price you will be able to execute at. Why?

Spread betting companies are like market makers in the real stock market. They 'make' a price on a financial market for you to trade. They are starting to provide some traders with what is called Direct Market Access (DMA), but in reality there are two entities which sit between you, the trader and the actual exchange, be it the London Stock Exchange, the Chicago Mercantile Exchange, NYMEX or even the wool market in Sydney. Although the exchange may publish an official price, and you may see this duplicated elsewhere, for example on a Bloomberg terminal, it is not the price you will trade on.

Between the exchange and the spread betting company sits another beast, usually an investment bank acting as a prime broker. A spread betting company may use several prime brokers to give it access to physical and futures markets in order to find the best price in the market. Some prime brokers are retained because they specialise in a particular market, and can procure the best price there. But ultimately, while you may feel like you are trading the market, and the price may be very similar to the one you are seeing quoted elsewhere, the price is ultimately the one your spread betting company chooses to quote you. *It is under no obligation to quote you the same price you are seeing in the market*; it will quote you the price of its product which tracks the market, but this will not be a product that matches the market point for point. Indeed, it is hard even for professionals to find a 'true' market price from their brokers.

Prime brokers will quote prices on markets to spread betting companies, but the price quoted by Deutsche Bank will not necessarily be the same price quoted by Goldman Sachs or Credit Suisse. They will be close, but not the same. The spread betting company then needs to come up with its own price, based on what it would theoretically get in the market. A good policy would be to aim for a price somewhere in the middle of those quoted by the prime brokers, but the spread betting company is under no obligation to do so, and depending on the level of automation involved in its pricing processes, you may see some substantial deviation from the spot price quoted in the market.

On top of this, you also have to factor in the spread – oh yes, those spreads again! As your spread betting company is quoting two prices, a bid and an offer, and each company has its own set of spreads, you can end up seeing some wide variations in prices, particularly during periods of high market volatility.

Finally, it is also worth remembering that the price quoted is not necessarily the price your order will be filled at. Again, it ought to be, and with very small trades it usually is. Suffice to say that if you find most of your trades are being filled at a different price from what you were quoted, it may be time to start looking for another broker!

Finding the right market for you

Not all markets suit all traders. Many successful traders will not only restrict themselves to a single area of investment, currencies for example, but they will also often focus on just one or two currency pairs. Some may only trade the oil price, day in, day out. There are hedge funds out there that devote all their time to trading oil or gas futures. This way they come to know one market extremely well. Other traders will hunt down price action, seeking markets where there are big daily moves, in order to profit from that. But again, to be successful, they make sure they understand those markets before they trade them, and that they also have a very good idea what is moving that price.

I have worked with hedge funds for many years now and have observed how successful hedge funds will focus on a very specific area of investment finance. One of the most successful commodities funds in the United States, which has consistently made money year in, year out, has achieved this by specialising in agricultural commodities, in particular the livestock futures market in Chicago. The fund's managers have a background in farming in the US, but in addition to this they have embraced new information flows (including looking at satellite photos of the American Midwest) which can give them a better perspective on what is happening in American farming, and how that information will affect livestock prices. Their edge is largely informational, but it has allowed them to beat the market consistently for almost two decades.

By contrast, global macro funds, hedge funds which dabble in many different markets, wherever they see an opportunity really, make sure they are fully informed about a market before they invest in it. Taking a position against the Malaysian rinngit (as George Soros famously did in 1997), is only done after very careful consideration of that market, and specialist teams of analysts and consultants are often hired to provide this expertise for the portfolio manager.

We obviously do not have such resources at our fingertips, but it is important to stress that a scattergun approach to spread betting is likely to end in tears. Maintaining internal discipline and divorcing yourself from your emotions is a critically important process in the making of a great trader. Let your human side talk to you too much, allow yourself to be distracted, and you will quickly find yourself starting to run up losses. This is not the market's fault; the market does not care. It is important that you develop a trading style, an approach that works for you and for your lifestyle and investment objectives. This way you will be able to get the most out of your spread betting experience.

Different types of spread bets

There are a number of different types of spread bet contract now available. Which you use will depend partly on what is being offered by your chosen provider, but also on what suits you best as a trader. As the spread betting industry has matured and evolved, so enterprising firms have sought new ways to accommodate their customers and win new business from their competitors. This has led to increasing product innovation in this space which may at times be confusing for the beginner. Don't be daunted however: once you have found the type of trade that suits you, you will probably find yourself sticking to it.

Futures spread bets

These were among the first type of spread bet to be offered. They are most suited to the medium- to long-term trader as they have a set expiry date (usually the end of March, June, September and December). They tend to have the widest spreads as well. When the spread bet expires – i.e. you get to midnight on the expiry date – you can usually roll it over to the next quarter. For the more short-term trader, there are also monthly contracts expiring at the end of every month.

Futures are exchange-traded contracts that traditionally were used to trade commodities. The idea was that the owner of the contract would be entitled to take delivery of that commodity – be it wheat, cattle, oil, frozen orange juice or something else – for the price of that futures contract when it expired. This was of particular value for those who wanted to seek to secure a commodity at a predictable price (an airline needing to buy fuel for its planes, for example).

These days, futures contracts are available on a lot more than just commodities. They can be based on stock market indexes, bond prices, shares, currencies, even interest rates. Futures are traditionally the province of big investors, like corporations, banks and hedge funds. But spread betting, while providing the private investor with access to the futures markets, lets you trade more cost-effectively, with smaller amounts of money.

Spread betting companies still use the futures prices as a guideline for the prices of the bets they quote, and consequently spread bets were initially structured in the same way, with an expiry date, based on a quarter or a month – e.g. Brent Crude March 2011.

Things are getting simpler now, but you will still see prices quoted with a month next to them. While you can roll over that trade into the next month or quarter with no problem if you so choose (you are not trading real futures here, and no one is going to deliver barrels of crude oil to your front garden if you forget to close a trade), you need to also be aware that prices of quarterly or monthly contracts will tend to converge on the spot price (the price of that market right now) as the contract gets closer to expiry.

When the contract is young – for example, a monthly spread bet on January crude oil which you might buy on 2 January – there is little real idea in the market of where the oil price is going to be on 31 January when that trade expires. As that date gets closer, the market starts to get more confident, and when you're within a day of expiry, the price of the monthly spread bet and the spot price will be very close indeed.

Some spread betting companies will only quote you the current contract, but some will also offer you a price on the next one, so for example, you could see both March and April Crude Oil on your screen. While rolling over your bet into the next contract will subject you to a financing charge, you usually won't be paying any other overnight financing charges while this contract is live.

Daily spread bets

These are short-term bets which expire at the end of the day. You can buy them at any point during the trading day, and they will tend to reflect the underlying cash market or spot price. They are easier to get to grips with than futures-based bets, but they do expire when the market closes. They obviously suit the more short-term trader who is looking at intra-day movements in the market.

Rolling spread bets

More recently, spread betting firms have been offering their clients rolling spread bets, effectively a daily bet which you are able to 'roll over' every night, usually for a small charge. Rolling spread bets let you keep your trade open indefinitely. They can get quite expensive over time, as the ongoing daily financing charges build up, but for the trader who is comfortable with a very short-term time horizon, they are quite useful.

There are other types of bets now being made available, some of which are exclusive to certain firms or are less widely available than those mentioned above.

Armed with our new understanding of financial spread betting, it is now time to look at how to go about choosing a spread betting company.

2

Finding the right spread betting company

Choosing the right spread betting company can be a bewildering process. Many firms are active advertisers at the moment, and are buying spaces in prominent locations, including billboards of major railway stations, in the business sections of national newspapers and online. At a time when many financial services companies are struggling, spread betting firms are continuing to make money.

There are now more companies offering spread betting services than ever before. The barriers to entry are lower, while the big, established firms are seeking ways to innovate, and to provide products and services that others cannot afford to deliver. In addition, the overall cost of trading is coming down as more firms seek to compete on price. For the new trader, this is a great time to be starting out, as many companies will bend over backwards to win your business.

Finally, many other companies are partnering with the big spread betting firms to offer 'white labelled' spread betting. These are usually banks and brokerages who don't want to go through the cost and effort of establishing their own spread betting operation, but are attracted by the idea of taking a slice of the profits. They can partner with a spread betting company that will offer them its pricing and execution facilities in exchange for access to their customer base. Many non-financial companies, like bookies and even newspapers, are jumping on this bandwagon.

For the consumer, as ever, it is important to read the small print. If your stock broker suddenly announces it can now offer you a spread betting account, this probably means it has signed a partnership agreement. The money in your account may – or may not – be held by the spread betting company, but it will be important to understand who your ultimate commercial arrangement is with, who is executing your trades and whose prices you are trading on.

In this chapter we look at how to make sense of the sometimes bewildering array of companies and products on offer. There are some independent websites that can help you with this, some of which I have listed at the back of this book, but in particular sites like The Armchair Trader (www. thearmchairtrader.com) can be helpful in sorting out who offers what.

A financial spread betting shopping list

Competition is hot out there right now, but not all spread betting companies offer the same suite of products and services. It is fair to say that some are better positioned to deal with the beginner than others.

For starters, some of the bigger companies have had the resources to invest in substantial educational programmes, which include colourful trading guides, videos, seminars and access to trading coaches who can answer your questions. These are usually offered free, and I would encourage you to take advantage of them.

Many spread betting companies use different trading 'platforms' – the system you use to place your trades, follow prices, even do some analysis on. These are getting more sophisticated all the time, so it is important that you familiarise yourself with a firm's trading platform before you go risking money on it. Much is made of these platforms, and indeed they can cost a considerable amount of time and money to build from scratch, so their creators can feel justly proud of them. But trading platforms are not the be-all and end-all. A poorly designed trading interface, however, can really cripple your ability to trade financial markets online. Spread betting companies will be able to take you through the process of familiarising yourself properly with the way their trading platform works, and it is essential that you do get to grips with it, or costly mistakes can occur later.

Spread betting education and trading platforms

A company's education programme will bring you up to speed not only on spread betting, but also on important aspects of it, like proper risk management. While it is great that the larger firms have taken this approach, it is also important to point out that they will never paint an entirely complete picture for you. The Financial Services Authority has, over the years, subtly prodded spread betting companies to highlight the risks involved in trading as an integral part of their marketing literature, and you should see risk warnings splattered all over their websites and advertisements. But, it is still worth getting an independent view and indeed, try spread betting without risking your money by using a demo account.

Free education is still, however, free education, and should be taken advantage of. Some very experienced former traders now work as analysts with the spread betting companies and regularly host free seminars, so it is worth keeping up to speed with what's on, both online and around the country. These events can also be a great opportunity to meet other traders and exchange notes.

Some, but not all, spread betting companies now offer what is called a demo account. This is an account using a limited number of markets with live prices that you can use to practise on. It has the advantage of letting you trade live, up-to-date market prices rather than delayed ones. Several firms now offer these, but some will only offer them for a limited period of time or with a restricted series of features. This is changing, however.

More sophisticated demo accounts are good news for the beginner. It means you can access a fully featured trading platform without putting up any cash. It also lets you try out the trading interface and test its functionality to see if you like it. I would not choose a firm based purely on whether its platform looks aesthetically pleasing on your computer screen, however, or makes a nice noise when you hit your limit order!

Some firms still require that an element of their trading software be downloaded onto your computer, even for a demo account. This can be a pain, particularly if you are on the move a lot, sometimes trade from the office, or use more than one computer. This situation is also changing, and the new generation of spread betting platforms do not require software installation, being accessible entirely from the web. They do, however, still need a decent broadband connection if you're going to take full advantage of them.

With the advent of mobile phone technology, in the last two years we have seen the launch of various mobile phone applications ('apps') that allow traders to follow markets and trade on the move. Obviously, there are limitations in terms of where you can do this (100 per cent mobile phone network coverage in the UK is still something we all dream of) and just how much functionality can currently be delivered to a mobile device. Applications will differ from provider to provider. Designing and implementing one effectively is no small task. Luckily, they are easy for firms to update with new patches which allow them be improved on an ongoing basis. Not all firms offer this level of accessibility to their trading platforms, so if trading on the move is important to you, it is worth bearing in mind.

Minimum account opening level

Next, look at how much firms are asking as a minimum account opening sum. This still varies quite widely. Some companies are not only set up to cater to novice traders, they are also equipped to service thousands of retail clients, even those only prepared to stake a maximum of a few hundred pounds. Others will only be interested in the big money traders. It is interesting to see the wide range of trades the dealing floor of a big firm will field in an average morning, with trades of a few pounds a point and others of hundreds of pounds a point being executed on the same market within seconds of each other. Minimum investment seems to be coming down all the time, however, as competition increases, and few firms will still insist on seeing £1,000 up front.

Related to this is the amount of money required to finance trades – i.e. the margin percentage. How much of the overall trade will the firm finance? This is partly dictated by that company's own capital situation. The richer they're feeling, the lower their margin rates will be. In the next chapter we will look more closely at the implication of margin rates, but suffice to say a low rate of margin is not always a good thing, particularly if you are a beginner.

Shopping around on price

When spread betting firms compete on price – and they are increasingly having to do this – they compete on the size of their spreads. In Chapter 1, we looked at how the spread is the difference between the price you buy at and the price you sell at. One of the ways spread betting companies make their money is by quoting a spread which is marginally wider than the spread they can get themselves in the market from their prime brokers. Fifteen years ago, when there were fewer spread betting companies competing in this space, they could afford to quote nice, fat spreads. Nowadays, spreads are getting narrower all the time, and according to some sources within the business, some spreads are now so narrow that firms have to be running some of these tight markets at a loss, in order to attract new business.

Behind all this is the fact that financial markets themselves are becoming more efficient. Across the board, in the most liquid markets, spreads are coming down as technology and fast communications make it harder for brokers to quote spreads well out of the market. These efficiencies are being passed on to the consumer as newer spread betting concerns seek to compete on price against those with more experience.

We are seeing record narrow levels in spreads on some key markets, like the big stock market indexes. These are already highly liquid markets, with plenty of volume in the futures markets, so spread betting firms can already afford to transfer this level of market activity to their customers in the form of tighter spreads.

Not all spread betting companies are convinced that competing on spreads is the way to go, and they quietly maintain the conviction that a shiny new trading platform or a bigger range of markets will still allow them to compete. Time – and the consumer – will tell.

Market range

The range of markets offered can be important to some traders. Much of the volume in trading at any given spread betting shop will be in a small handful of key, headline markets. These include the big financial indexes, the most important currency pairs, and the commodities that are most closely followed by the media, economists and global trading desks. Indeed, 80 per cent or more of the volume of trading in any given month will be accounted for by fewer than a dozen markets.

This means most of the traders, and most of the money, are focusing on the same prices. These are the markets where spread betting companies will be competing most aggressively when it comes to hacking down spreads and margins. Outside these markets, the pricing will not necessarily be as competitive.

There are other factors at work behind the scenes determining what spreads a firm can offer, but this issue seems to produce more heated arguments between marketers and senior management at spread betting companies than any other!

Outside the popular instruments, however, there is now a wide range of markets available to trade, including some emerging markets' currencies and indexes, exchange traded funds, commodity baskets and an expanding range of commodities markets. In addition, some firms are also seeking to deliver 'proprietary' trading products based on futures prices; for example, spread bets based on company sectors, where the price is determined by the underlying share prices of the companies that compose that sector in the FTSE 350.

The types of bet offered can also be important. 'Vanilla bets' are standard, basic spread bets but not all types of bets are offered by all spread betting companies.

Leading firms will also make much of the fact that they have received independent recognition from the financial media for their products or services. Having worked many years in the financial media myself, and been involved with a number of awards ceremonies, I'd advise the consumer to take these with a pinch of salt. They tend to favour the established players, particularly those with the most lavish advertising budgets.

While it is true that deeper pockets can also provide superior products and services to the trader, this is not always the case. However, publishers of financial magazines always need to have one eye on their bottom line, and glitzy black tie awards ceremonies, while making everyone feel good about themselves, also contribute heavily to magazines' P&L (Profit & Loss). My advice to the beginning trader: don't be guided by how many awards a company has won. Marketing departments love to plaster them all over their advertising, but the proof of the pudding, as always, is in the eating.

Astute traders will use more than one spread betting account. The primary reason for doing so is to allow proper comparison of the spreads and prices between the two. If a trader is focusing in particular on a handful of markets, he can develop a good idea of where a price should be, and place trades with the firm that can offer the most competitive prices most consistently. While this is less of an issue for the beginner, it is worth considering further down the line if you have the spare capital to commit to a second account.

How do they make their money?

Financial spread betting can be extremely lucrative for the firms involved, and there are always suspicions, perpetuated by online traders' bulletin boards and investing forums, that the markets quoted by the brokerages are somehow rigged, or that sales desks are taking advantage of their knowledge of clients' positions, particularly their stop losses, to make money at their expense. The lack of any obvious fees being charged for all the expensive software, training and other facilities which firms seemingly offer for nothing can also make potential customers wonder how all this can be afforded in the first place.

The two main areas of income for spread betting firms are the financing side of the operation, and the spreads. Beyond that, there are other sources of profit, but these are generally minor compared to the main income streams.

Spreads quoted to clients will usually be slightly wider than the spreads in the underlying market. A firm that quotes a six point spread on a share price might be able to access that same spread, should it wish to hedge its position, at four points. It is making a point of profit either side, which it realises when the trade is opened and when it is closed.

On this basis, spread betting firms make money on volume – i.e. the more people trade, the more money the firm will make. It is important to understand that for most spread betting companies, whether you make money or not is neither here nor there. It is whether you trade in the first place.

Stories of spread betting firms betting against their clients have some basis in fact, but are really the province of some of the more unethical firms out

Table 2.1: Spreads on typical spread betting markets, 2011 (points)

UK 100	1
US 30	1
Euro 50	2
Japan 225	15
Hong Kong 43	12
Arcelor Mittal	0.0428
Citigroup	0.030
Reed Elsevier	0.0190
GBP/USD	0.00010
EUR/USD	0.00009
USD/JPY	0.009
EUR/CHF	0.00020
Gold	0.40
Silver	0.030
Soybean	0.150
Sugar	0.050
Eurodollar 3 month	0.01

Note: This list is based on typical spreads being quoted by leading companies in the sector in July 2011. Spreads tend to vary more frequently than margin rates, and can even fluctuate sometimes in the course of the trading day.

there that have been tempted into crossing the line in the past. The nature of today's financial regulatory regime coupled with the increased competition in the sector, means that those firms that feel they can consistently cheat their clients will not stay in business for long. Go online and do some research, and you will get an indication of the current reputations – good or bad – of the various companies offering spread betting.

Spread betting companies are also in the business of lending money. The very fact that they offer margin trading facilities means they are offering credit. When opening a live account with a spread betting company, you are entering into a credit agreement. The company concerned will analyse your financial circumstances, just as a mortgage lender would, to assess whether you can afford to trade in the first place. You will be bound by UK credit legislation and regulations as surely as if you were borrowing money to buy a car.

Spread betting companies in turn borrow money from banks to do this lending. How cheaply they can afford to do so is based on their existing capital base and their credit agreements with their banks. But be sure: the rates at which they lend to traders on the long side of bets will be higher than they borrow from their bank. Conversely, the rate they borrow from traders on the short side will be lower than they could get from placing money in the interbank market.

Think of a spread betting company like a bank: they can ensure they have a relatively steady income from lending and borrowing, making money on the difference between the interbank rates and the rates they quote their customers. It can be very profitable.

On top of this, firms can also make money from the overnight financing charge they levy for customers who keep trades open outside normal trading hours. The introduction of rolling daily bets and its subsequent popularity has increased the scope for companies to make money from this credit line.

Beyond this, spread betting companies can make money from trading themselves. Their activities in this respect will tend not to have any impact on the profitability of their clients, but they can see when many clients are all taking the same position. Usually, a firm will be able to 'net' its client positions off against each other: for example, if I am long Vodafone, someone else spread betting with the same company could be short Vodafone. All that the dealer sitting at his desk in the City needs to worry about is that the company can make money off the spread. Sometimes, when this is not the case, and there are not enough 'opposite' positions to net off, the firm will hedge out the risk in the underlying market with futures contracts.

However, in a case where a large number of clients are behind a trade which the spread betting firm believes will lose money (and when you're as close to the market as they are, it can be obvious at times), they can simply opt not to hedge those positions. In this case, if the clients turn out to be wrong, the spread betting firm will profit. I would stress that this is simply a proprietary trading tactic, a situation where a firm sees an opportunity to make money on its own book by simply electing not to hedge, as it normally might. It is taking on a degree of risk itself by doing this, and could lose money if its clients turn out to be right.

If you spend all day working on the dealing floor of a spread betting firm, you do end up developing a good feeling for where the market is going to go under some circumstances, and then, when you see several client trades arriving, taking the opposite view, you do tend to wonder what they're up to. I remember one morning where early on in the day a small number of clients took aggressive long positions on Lloyds TSB at a point in time where I thought the stock would fall, and potentially quite far. My assumption was they must know something I didn't. As it turned out, they didn't, and they lost quite a lot of money by lunchtime. I don't know what the firm's net position was on Lloyd's at that point, but if the senior traders had shared my view, they might have elected not to hedge on the short side and taken some profit for the firm.

There are also some fairly endemic suspicions among traders as regards the practice of 'requotes'. This is where you are quoted a price and trade on the basis of that price, but then end up with the trade being executed at a marginally different price. This could be because the market is moving fast, and the dealing desk has not been able to execute quickly enough. Rather than wear the difference themselves, they pass on the difference to the client. This may not seem like a lot of money if you are trading at a couple of pounds per point, but those who see themselves losing hundreds of pounds this way, on a regular basis, probably have a right to be angry.

If this was seen to work in favour of the client 50 per cent of the time, there would probably be fewer complaints, but some spread bettors continue to argue that the brokers are always requoting in favour of the firm, not the client. It has led to a great deal of bad blood between the trading community and some spread betting firms, but due to the lack of empirical evidence, this is hard to prove either way.

As the world of global financial markets moves into the era of high frequency trading, where increasingly computers are being tasked to execute trades in the space of milliseconds – i.e. faster than any human being could possibly react – the issue of requotes should recede. Already some firms are using extremely sophisticated trading programs to manage client orders and ensure that the price you trade at is the price you execute at, even when markets are quite lively.

My view is that firms which continue to requote trades on a consistent basis will not be able to remain in business. It is a big issue for traders, and they will vote with their feet if they feel they are being short-changed.

What about CFDs?

You will see many spread betting firms also advertising products called contracts for difference, or CFDs. These are very similar derivatives products to spread bets, although there are some essential differences. CFDs allow you to trade many of the same financial markets online as you can with a spread bet. However, they are not tax free in the UK, and the risk you take on with them is measured slightly differently.

CFDs are subject to capital gains tax in the UK, which also means you can off-set losses you sustain as a consequence of trading them against your total tax bill. But your profits can also be taxed as well. There are very few reasons to trade CFDs if you are UK resident, but some traders still prefer to trade them.

One reason may be that CFDs don't use the 'per point' stake system of spread bets. They are priced just like other financial instruments, like shares, although you can still trade them on margin, like spread bets.

CFDs evolved as financial products for banks, fund managers and other institutional investors, but they are now widely advertised to the retail investing public. Outside the British Isles and the US, CFDs are the default structure used for online margin trading. They have become particularly popular in markets like Germany and Australia, where there is no spread betting, although they are not currently available in the US.

CFDs are becoming more widely acceptable by global regulators – for example, some Canadian provinces are now close to authorising them for retail distribution. As a non-UK or Irish trader, your mostly likely alternative to spread bets will be CFDs.

What about advisory spread betting services?

Like advisory stock broking services, advisory CFD trading or spread betting is also marketed fairly heavily in the UK, particularly by brokerages that may also offer advisory share dealing. These arrangements may sound attractive, as they offer the newcomer an 'experienced' voice on the end of the phone who can recommend potential trades. These firms will likely have preferential dealing terms with one or more of the big spread betting companies. They will charge a fee for their advice as well as the opportunity to execute trades.

Even experienced traders like to bounce their ideas off others from time to time. They like to have another person to act as a sanity check on what they are doing. An advisory broker is not, however, the right person to do this for you. Ultimately, they are conflicted. It is a rare broker who is going to tell you to stay out of the market because it is too choppy. They make money when you trade, whether you win or lose. Their business depends on you taking on more risk, and they will tend to advise you to trade more frequently than you need to, in the interests of earning more fees for themselves.

Needless to say, there are innumerable tales of woe out there from investors who have lost money with advisory firms. Frequently, the advice is to take positions using single share spread bets, which can go horribly wrong quite quickly. You are also relying heavily on your advisor to time your entry and exit from the market and limit your risk, which is asking a lot, particularly for a small account (anything up to £50,000).

At the end of the day, most of the most talented hedge fund managers and traders of the past three decades did not cut their teeth in advisory brokerages. Anyone with a modicum of serious investment talent is not going to be staffing the sales desk of a retail brokerage with £10,000 trade tickets to place. They will be on the trading desk of a multi-billion dollar hedge fund. Yes, there are some good advisory brokers out there, and I don't want to tar an entire industry with the same brush, but it can cost you a lot of money before you find one.

In the post-credit crunch environment, where there is more emphasis than ever before on DIY investing, I would suggest educating yourself about risks and opportunities in the financial markets, and not relying on someone else to do it for you. If you want someone to be on hand to counsel you during your trading week, there are some excellent trading coaches out there who will, for a fee, fill this role. Note that they will charge you a flat fee for their advice, and can often help you to shape a strategy that suits your personality and risk tolerance. They are not there to manage your money for you, or to make money every time you place a trade. There is a big difference between a trading coach and an advisory broking service.

3

Risk management for the margin trader

Risk should always be foremost in the mind of the online trader. When traders get a position wrong, be they private traders or the professionals, more often than not it is because they get their risk management wrong. Many, many investors who plunge into financial spread betting pay little attention to risk, or simply do not understand the sorts of risks they are taking on. They end up losing money, become down-hearted, close their accounts and go on to do something else.

Spread betting is not like investing in a mutual fund. Opening a trade and letting it run without having adequate built in protection can cost you a lot of money. Nobody else is going to pay attention to your active positions. It is up to you to come up with an adequate risk framework and to go from there.

Professional money managers spend a lot of time talking about risk, seeking to quantify it, and using phrases like 'dial up on the risk' or 'taking risk off the table'. You may also read in the financial press about the market becoming more 'risk averse'. Trading financial markets is all about confidence and awareness of risk. The last thing you want, as a trader, is to be ambushed by an unforeseen risk.

A recent famous incident involved a large hedge fund that bought futures based on Japan's Nikkei 225 index, shortly after the March 2011 earthquake struck the country. The index had already fallen sharply, and the Swiss-based fund manager felt it was under-priced and could now be bought. Although not a split second decision, it was a bet that failed to take into consideration the possibility that the earthquake would also create a tsunami. By the time the tidal wave struck Miyagi prefecture, the hedge fund in question was already long the Nikkei 225, as it went on to plunge some more and cost the manager US$300 million. In this scenario, the trader thought he was aware of all the risks, but had overlooked a large and highly significant threat to his position.

Margin trading

Financial spread betting involves trading on margin. We discussed the basics of margin trading earlier in this book, but it pays to revisit the inherent risks involved in trading on margin, as this sets spread betting apart from investing in shares or investment trusts.

Margin trading in effect means borrowing money to trade. Imagine if a bank lent you money to trade rather than buy a new car. The bank says it will let you pocket any profits or losses. By lending you £25,000, it allows you to make bigger profits – or losses – than you would be able to with £2,500.

Margin trading works very like this. The bank here is the financial spread betting company. It asks you to provide a portion of the trade – say 10 per cent – and it effectively 'lends' you the rest. Spread betting companies pay a lot of attention to the creditworthiness of their clientele and for obvious reasons: if someone loses more money than they have on deposit with the firm, they want to be sure that the trader can still cover his losses.

Spread betting companies set margin rates that will differ depending upon the market or share price. To a large extent, the rate reflects the cost to the spread betting company of hedging its underlying risk in the market. The more liquid the market, the lower the margin is likely to be. Liquidity is a very important consideration for the online trader: it represents how easy it is to buy and sell something in the market. While spread betting, you are not really trading real market prices, but at the same time the overall market liquidity will have an impact on the margin you have to deposit.

Most spread betting firms will quote fixed margins for most markets, although this can change, and at short notice, if something affects the liquidity of the share or market you are spread betting. Usually, fixed spreads will be quoted on markets like currencies, commodities, and bonds, as well as indexes, and these are unlikely to change. Spreads on shares, particularly the less liquid shares, can change and change suddenly. The lower margin markets will tend to be the most liquid. Thus, you should see 1–5 per cent margin asked for forex markets, some commodities and stock market indexes. These markets are very liquid, as they are based on the huge volumes traded in futures every day.

In addition, it can be difficult to make money on markets where daily changes are incremental, unless you are using considerable amounts of margin. Foreign exchange markets are typical examples, as daily changes are relatively small compared to shares. Hence, FX traders need lower margin rates in order to make any money at all. A 1:1 currency trade is not going to make you an awful lot of money. Think about how much money you made with your remaining foreign currency last time you came back from holiday.

At the other end of the margin scale will be smaller shares, which may only see a handful of trades in the physical market every week, and hence will see higher margin levels, to the tune of as much as 50 per cent (in which case the spread betting company is lending you a pound for every pound of your own).

On the face of it, margin trading sounds like a great idea. After all, your bank is unlikely to lend you money to gamble with. And you are only risking a small fraction of the total trade, yet you get to keep all the profits.

The problem here is that you also wear the losses. Think of a margin trade like a high performance sports car – you can drive a lot faster, but when you crash, you are risking life and limb! That is why all spread betting companies are obliged to publish risk warnings on their marketing literature and their websites. It is therefore essential to keep a close eye on how trading margin can affect your profits and losses.

Figure 3.1 illustrates how margin can turbo-charge the potential profits you can make from a trade, in this case using just 20 per cent margin to trade a share. The column on the left is the trade using the physical share on the stock market, with no margin involved. The column on the right is the trade with the margin factored in – i.e. a typical spread bet. Here we are assuming a small gain in the share of 5 per cent – you can see how, with margin trading, your profit potential is magnified.

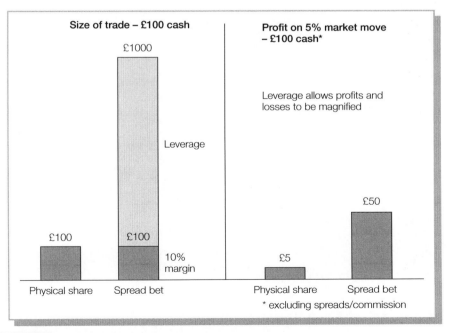

Figure 3.1   **Profit potential of margin trading**

Now imagine that same trade in reverse. Figure 3.2 gives you some idea of what a 5 per cent loss would look like. The third column illustrates the total 'weight' or risk you are wearing. You can see that by margin trading you are effectively 'owning' a much bigger amount of risk. The spread betting company may be lending you the money to bet with, but the profit or loss is all yours, come what may.

Consequently, spread betting requires much closer day-to-day monitoring of your positions, and this is why many traders prefer to close out all their positions when they go away on holiday, or even when they go to sleep. They don't like to have the additional psychological pressure of open trades to keep them awake.

I know of one professional floor trader in the United States who forgot to close out a long position in the coffee futures market on a Friday. He only remembered when he got back to his trading desk after the market had opened. Luckily for him, by that stage the price had gone in his favour, and

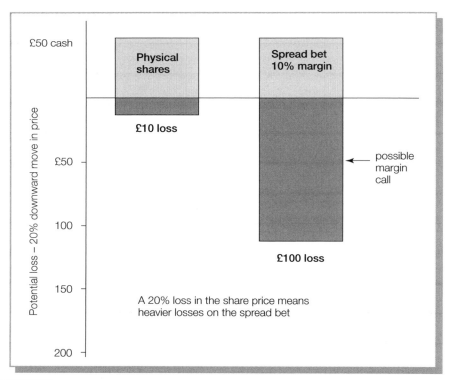

Figure 3.2   **The downside to margin trading (at 10 per cent margin)**

he was up $250,000 in a weekend, but he ruefully admitted that had it gone the other way, it would have 'ruined his day' (and probably his marriage!)

Stop losses

Most spread betting companies should now provide you with the ability to place 'stop losses'. They will let you insert an automatic sell order when you open the bet, or indeed later on (some are now insisting that traders automatically have a stop loss in place when they open a trade).

The stop loss sets the price at which the company will close the bet, and is often used as a key tool in risk management. It means you have a degree of peace of mind: your bet will not keep losing you money; at some point it will be closed. It lets you define how much money you are prepared to lose on a given bet.

It is important, when putting a stop in place, that you do not place it too close to where you opened the trade. Otherwise you can quickly be 'stopped out' of that trade when you don't really need to be.

Figure 3.3 shows an example of a typical week in the life of the FTSE 100 index – or a typical bet on the UK 100 index – with one of the spread betting firms. You can also see how a trade has been opened on the Monday morning, and two hypothetical stops have been put in place.

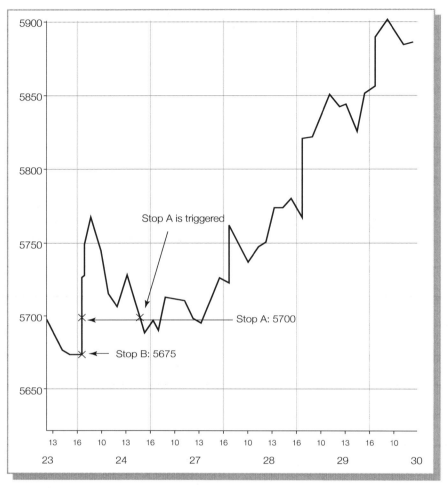

© IT-Finance.com

Figure 3.3 **Placing stop losses**

Stop A was too close to the index, and in this case the trader gets stopped out too early and loses out on some of the potential profits he could pocket later in the week. Stop B involves the trader taking on more risk, because his potential loss would be bigger, but at the same time his stop does not get hit, and he goes on to make money.

Assessing where to place stops really depends on the volatility of the market you are betting on, and the timescale you are using. Not only does the volatility of markets change constantly, but some markets are inherently more volatile than others. Some traders love volatile markets, because they feel they can make more money when the price is moving in big jumps, while others seek out steady, consistent trends over a period of days or weeks.

It is important that you have a good feel for the potential price jumps of a market you are trading. Think about your timescale first. Are you a short-term trader or a longer-term trader? How long do you expect the bet to be open, and do you have any particular target price you would like to reach?

Then look at what the price of that market has done over that timescale, but go back further too. How has it behaved? Think of it as if it were a person. What does its temperament look like? Is it subject to sudden and unpredictable jumps? Even if you expect to be in the market for no more than a week, it is worth tracking back several weeks to see where the price has gone in the past. You don't want to be surprised by a sudden change of mood, even if the last temper tantrum was a few weeks or even months ago. This is no guarantee of future market behaviour, of course, but it can provide useful information about where to place your stops without them being hit immediately.

Figure 3.4 provides us with another example, this time of the S&P 500. You can see how, by looking back over a period of a couple of months, the trader can assess whether the price is likely to move suddenly, and place his stops accordingly.

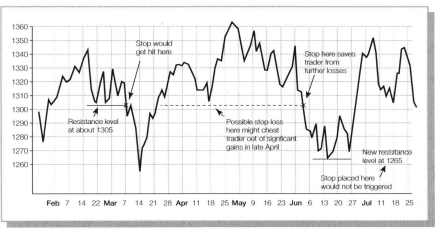

© StockCharts.com
$SPX (S&P 500 Large Cap Index) INDX 28-Jul-2011 $SPX (Daily)

Figure 3.4   **Informed stop losses**

Placing stop losses can also be informed by technical analysis. We will look at this in more detail in Chapter 8, but technical analysis can certainly help to keep you abreast of where to put your stops. You can see from looking at Figure 3.4 that the share hits a number of resistance levels, both on the way up and on the way down. We will discuss resistance levels in more detail in Chapter 8, but suffice to say resistance levels are predictable turning points in a given price. They can also help you when deciding where to put your stop losses.

When is a stop loss *really* a stop loss?

Bear in mind that a stop loss does not guarantee that your trade will be closed at that price. The spread betting company will use that stop loss as an indicator, and will try to close the bet as soon as it can once that price point is reached. Only if the company offers its clients *guaranteed* stop losses can you expect to see trades closed at the price you want.

Some traders complain vociferously about trades not being closed efficiently. This really boils down to a question of quality of service more than anything else. As the technological infrastructure underpinning the way spread betting companies manage their client accounts becomes more efficient, I expect to see more firms offering guaranteed stop losses as a standard part of their service package.

The other big complaint is that companies deliberately stop their clients out: the argument here is that spread betting companies might know that a large number of clients have stops in place at a certain level, and can 'twitch' the price down far enough to trigger all the stops. This does happen in the real market from time to time, and because the prices you bet on are the prices of the spread betting company itself, *not* the real market (although an effort is made to keep them as close together as possible), there is always a suspicion in the minds of some traders that they are being deliberately stopped out.

I cannot say for certain that this practice happens regularly in spread betting; I've certainly not seen it happen myself. Ultimately, spread betting companies will make money if they see more volume, not if they punish their customers' risk management strategies. They are waking up to the fact that an unhappy customer is a customer who won't trade with them any longer. The days of 'churn and burn' in spread betting are fast disappearing. However, if you feel unhappy with the service you are getting from a firm on your stop losses, take it up with them, or close your account and trade with someone else.

Trailing stop losses are coming into increasing use in this industry, and represent a potentially profitable innovation for traders. With a trailing stop the stop loss moves behind the price. You simply decide how far behind. This way you can potentially lock in profits once the trailing stop has passed the point where you entered the market. If the price falls back, it will hit the stop at a much higher level than if it was merely static.

Figure 3.5 illustrates the difference between a trailing stop and a static stop, using the FTSE 100. Be aware that the spreads on some bets can widen suddenly, for example on shares at the beginning of the day. Not all spreads will remain the same all the time, particularly if you are trading share prices as opposed to markets with more predictable liquidity like foreign exchange and the big commodities. If your stop loss is too close, a sudden widening of the spread, for example at the beginning of the trading day in the share markets, can trigger your stop.

Some markets are also subject to overnight 'gapping'. This means that while the market may have closed at one price the day before, overnight news, particularly of an unexpected nature, can move the price suddenly as soon as the market opens (for example, afternoon developments in US markets can severely affect the opening of European markets the next day). Many, many stops get triggered this way and it can sometimes be quite hard for spread betting companies to get you out at the price you want when there is such a sudden shift in the underlying market. Be cautious then,

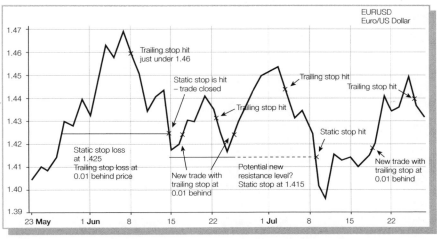

www.LiveCharts.co.uk

Figure 3.5   **Trailing stop versus static stop**

particularly when trading companies or markets where there is constant newsflow affecting their price (e.g. if there are major challenges to management, a takeover, or financial or regulatory difficulties).

One other important point to bear in mind when using stop losses: some firms' trading platforms can also treat the stop as an order to open a new trade, so be sure that, once you close a bet manually, the stop is also closed. Otherwise, if your live trade is gone, and the stop is still there, and the price moves through it, a new trade can be opened automatically. It may sound silly, but it pays to be sure.

Let's say you were long the FTSE (UK 100), and had a stop loss in place, but then saw the market coming off yourself and decided to close the bet. With some companies, if the FTSE then fell through your still-existing stop, a short trade would then open and you would be live in the market with a short position.

Under these circumstances, you would be notified as per usual that a new trade was live, but it is very important that you are familiar with the way stop losses are treated by the firm you are trading with in order to avoid this. Some firms cancel stops when you close the bet, others don't.

Managing your exposure

It is absolutely critical, when trading on margin, that you have sufficient cash to cover any losses you take. This means not just the deposit, but any other losses that might occur. After all, one of the big differences between spread betting and trading assets in the physical market – like listed shares or investment trusts for example – is that you really can lose more money than you put up. If things go badly, £100 of initial risk can quickly turn into a much larger loss, particularly if there are no stops in place, and the market turns suddenly and unexpectedly against you.

Each firm will also calculate its margin requirement differently. Increasingly, spread betting firms are keeping their customers abreast of what their total margin requirement is. This will be the amount of money you will need to have on deposit to meet your share of an open trade.

Some spread betting firms will use winning trades or other positions as positive factors in calculating your total margin requirement, others will factor in any stops you have in place, but it is best to ask what the margin policy is before diving in, particularly if your total margin requirement is not immediately apparent on your trading screen. Increasingly, more spread betting firms are reporting total margin required on a real-time basis, which is a big help for traders who can't take the time out to calculate their margin every couple of hours. It can become increasingly complicated if several positions are open at the same time.

Your margin will change as the value of open positions changes. If you start losing money, your spread betting company is entitled to ask you to deposit more cash in your account ('a margin call'). If you don't, or are unable to, then they are within their rights to start closing your positions themselves and saddling you with a loss.

Most experienced traders will keep a substantial amount of cash in their account ready to meet the margin requirements of any trades which might start losing ground. What they don't do is risk 80 per cent of their trading capital as margin on open trades and hope for the best. Trading requires discipline, and it does require trading capital for this very reason.

Spread betting companies always advise clients not to risk money that they cannot afford to lose. It helps with a trader's peace of mind if he knows he can get wiped out, and it won't have a knock on effect on his lifestyle! Ploughing your life savings or university money into a trading account in the hopes of growing it quickly almost always ends in tears.

It is also worth getting out of the market from time to time, partly from a psychological perspective, but also if you are going to be out of touch with your computer for an extended period of time. I know of one Swiss-based trader who routinely closes out all her positions at the end of June and then goes travelling around Asia for a couple of months, every year. This lets her get away from the markets at a time when they're relatively quiet, but at the same time she can do some important thinking about the strategies she employs, and she always finds she can bring something new to her approach when she returns to Switzerland in the autumn.

Mobile trading applications are making it easier for traders to keep tabs on their positions on the move, but these are no excuse for poor risk management. Any serious break from the markets should include 'going to cash' and exiting all positions. It means you don't have to worry about bad things happening to your account while you are away, and you can relax on the beach without having to steal a glance at the markets every day (unless you want to, of course).

When starting out, then, it is worth only ever having one or two positions open at the same time, and making sure you keep abreast of what your margin exposure is on a day-by-day basis.

Position sizing

Seasoned spread bettors will not risk all their money in active trades. Indeed, they will tend to commit only a tiny proportion of the money they have on deposit with the broker – as little as 1–3 per cent. This means an account with £5,000 might only be using £150 on a single live bet. This is sometimes referred to as the Pot Risk Rule. It is designed to protect you against a string of bad losses.

It seems very conservative to be risking only £150 at a time when have you £5,000 sitting in your account, but this is the reality of good risk management in today's spread betting world. Under this rule, if you lost that £150, you would then have only £4,850 to bet with. Your next maximum trade would be around £145. As you can see, if you were particularly unlucky, and took a string of hits to your trading capital, you would be risking progressively less on each trade. What you would *not* be doing is putting more risk on the table in order to make up for previous losses – this is the road to eventual trading disaster.

Under this scenario, it may seem like it will take you forever to make any money spread betting, and certainly that dream of perhaps one day trading by the pool of your villa in Spain may seem even further out of reach, but bear in mind you are also using leverage here. Even with £150, at 1 per cent margin your total market position would be £15,000!

Position sizing also helps you to evaluate your stop losses. If you are betting with a maximum loss per trade of £150, you will be able to see which markets are too volatile for your current risk tolerance. You don't want to be spread betting in a market which regularly sweeps through 100 points if you are betting £2 per point.

Not all bets are created equal

When spread betting, you are allocating risk by adding a number of pounds per point the price changes. So, £1 per point on the UK 100, for example, will involve less risk than £5 a point. However, you must also be aware of the hidden risk when betting on a different market. For instance, £1 a point on the UK 100 is not the same as £1 a point on Vodafone. Not all trades are created equal. Why?

Table 3.1 shows an example of how a £1/point bet in four different financial spread betting markets can represent a substantially different level of risk. I have included examples of two different shares as well. While it may

Table 3.1: Different exposure results from a £1 per point spread bet

Market	Price	10% Price Move	Effect on £1/point spread bet
UK 100	5499.3	549.9	£5499
Danske Bank	69.41	0.694	£694
USD/JPY	78.018	7.802	£7802
Natural Gas	3.645	0.365	£365

feel that you are just risking the same amount of money, in reality you are not. Even before margin is factored in, your total level of exposure on each bet differs substantially.

Every time you open a bet, it is important that you are aware of your total exposure. This is less of a problem if you intend to only trade UK 100, or the oil market. But if you are planning to spread bet on the prices of individual shares, for example, then you need to be aware of how your total exposure from share to share will vary. Every share is different when it comes to spread betting.

Make sure you have a back-up plan

Beyond the risks you take on with margin trading in the market, there are also additional, unforeseen risks that might have an impact on your trading strategy, and for which it can be useful to have a plan. What happens, for example, if you lose your internet connection, or you spill your coffee on your computer and it shorts out? What is your back-up plan?

It is worth thinking about these key risks early on, so that you have a plan in place should something like this happen. Problems with technology are often cited, but there are also other questions such as your own ability to trade. What happens if you are taken ill suddenly, with live positions in the market? Is anyone authorised to close your trades for you if this happens?

If your spread betting firm – your counterparty in industry parlance – should fail, it is worth knowing what your recourse is. After the events of 2008, when queues formed outside branches of the Northern Rock building society, many traders and investors became much more cautious about who their counterparties were. In the wake of the collapse of Lehman Brothers, it seems as if no financial institution is theoretically too big to fail and, as a trader, you won't know which banks your spread betting company is exposed to.

The best protection under these circumstances is to use more than one counterparty and, if you can afford it, split your trading cash up between them. It will mean you can't trade some markets, which have to be a bit tighter in terms of your overall margin, but this is no bad thing, particularly for the beginner.

When spread betting companies fail

Under normal market conditions, it is unlikely that spread betting companies will fail, but under extreme circumstances, as we saw in 2008, they can get into difficulties with their own creditors, and can collapse.

Echelon Fund Management was a Glasgow-based spread betting firm which collapsed in 2008 with debts of more than £30 million as its credit lines were severed. This was happening to a lot of companies in 2008, not just spread betting firms, but in the case of Echelon, it was forced to close its doors when a major creditor in Switzerland turned off the taps.

Approximately 900 Echelon clients ended up as creditors of the now-insolvent spread betting firm. Under these circumstances, because Echelon was regulated by the UK regulator, the Financial Services Authority, its spread betting clients were entitled to recompense to the tune of up to £48,000 each. This is because spread betting companies in the UK are covered by the Investors Compensation Scheme (ICS).

Smaller spread betting concerns are also more vulnerable to big losses being run up by their own clients. Spread betting companies will sometimes have blue chip clients who trade large sums of money. They need to keep a close eye on them, because it is possible for large losses sustained by a single customer to bring down the whole firm, as happened to Global Trader Europe in 2008. In the case of GTE, the losses caused a shortfall in the minimum amount of regulatory capital, which the firm is obliged to keep on deposit to meet FSA requirements. Its South African parent company took the decision not to continue to support it, forcing it out of business.

Smaller firms are much more prone to collapse than their bigger cousins, and it seems that periods of market volatility and uncertainty can increase this risk. However, it is also worth pointing out that the bigger firms have sailed through a number of major financial crises in one piece. On average, spread betting companies tend to be over-capitalised – i.e. they have more cash on account than other parts of the UK financial services industry. This is due to the nature of the business they are involved in.

Having said that, the slew of new entrants to the spread betting game means there are now more smaller players than there used to be. If opening an account with a smaller firm, it is worth asking some searching questions about who they are, who owns them, who is making the prices you will be betting on and where your money is being held.

The ICS covers investors for the first £30,000 they are owed, and then 90 per cent of the next £20,000. The scheme is financed by the investment firms themselves, rather than the government, but it ensures that, in the event of the collapse of a spread betting firm under the burden of its own debts, its customers can still claw their money back. It can be tougher, of course, for those who lend to spread betting companies.

Client money held by spread betting companies is ring-fenced, as it would be with a normal stock broker. In the event of the failure of the spread betting company, the money is distributed back to the clients according to the usual insolvency procedures, but this can take time, and the firms brought in for the purpose are not always good at communicating with creditors.

Summary: core principles of spread betting risk management

Most elements of effective risk management are based on common sense. I have summarised them below. Once you become more familiar with spread betting, and begin managing multiple positions, or adding to existing ones, then it behoves you to bring in more complex proprietary calculations to figure out what your total risk is. This can be hard to do, but it is an important discipline, as it allows you to make more informed trading decisions.

Risk management: the key points

1 Don't trade with money you cannot afford to lose
2 Make sure you can cover not only your initial margin, but also substantial additional margin for losing positions
3 Don't trade markets you don't understand
4 Always be aware of how much exposure you are taking on when you open a trade

5   Always use a stop loss

6   Be aware of how much money you could lose before your stop is hit

7   A stop loss is not a guaranteed stop loss unless your spread betting company says it is – sudden changes in the market can also catch spread betting firms off-balance

8   Consider trading with more than one spread betting company, even if it limits the amount of total margin you can take on

9   Make sure the firm you are spread betting with is properly regulated by the Financial Services Authority, entitling you to protection from the Investors Compensation Scheme

10 Make sure you have a disaster recovery plan in place, if you lose your internet connection or are taken ill suddenly.

4

Spread betting on shares and indexes

Spread betting with equity indexes

Stock market indexes are one of the first financial markets that novice spread bettors are encouraged to learn with. This is because they are more familiar to the average investor, being regularly quoted in the media and in the business press. Many major share markets have at least one benchmark index to represent the fortunes of that country's stock market. They are fairly easy to understand: their performance, up or down, is intended to reflect the average performance of the shares of the companies that make up that index.

Spread betting companies offer their clients a broad range of stock market indexes to trade with, including all the major markets. However, you will rarely see them described as the FTSE 100 or Dow Jones Industrial Average on your trading screen. Instead, you may have seen the UK 100, or the Germany 30.

Where indexes differ, is in how they are constructed. How many companies can be included? How often are they re-balanced? How much influence do the larger companies have over the overall performance of the index? Heavy buying or selling in particular companies or sectors can have a major influence, on a day-to-day basis, on the performance of an index.

To use an index as the basis for a financial product, as a financial company you need to pay the owner of the index a licence fee. Hence, firms that launch index-tracking products will typically pay a licence fee to the firm that is responsible for calculating and managing that index. FTSE International, for example, owns the FTSE series of indexes. Hence, instead of the indexes themselves, you might see something similar to the contents of Table 4.1 on your trading platform.

Spread betting firms are not claiming that their products are tracking the index. Indeed, they do not track them completely perfectly. Always remember, when you are betting on an index product with a spread bet company, the prices you are using belong to that company. They are not the real price of that index in the market. They are similar, but not perfectly aligned, which is why a particular market may be called the UK 100 – it tracks the prices of the top 100 UK shares quoted by the spread betting company. It looks a bit like the FTSE 100. It even behaves very similarly to the FTSE 100, but at the end of the day, it is *not* the FTSE 100.

It is in the interests of the spread betting company to make sure that price parity is close, otherwise traders will lose confidence in the price they are

Table 4.1 Popular spread betting indexes and their real world equivalents

Spread bet	Index
UK 100	FTSE 100
UK 250	FTSE 250
US 30	Dow Jones Industrial Average
US 500	S&P 500
Germany 30	DAX
France 40	CAC
Euro 50	EuroStoxx 50
Japan 225	Nikkei 225
Tech 100	NASDAQ Composite
Australia 200	ASX

getting. Efficiency of pricing and execution are becoming key competitive edges in this industry, and traders will walk away when they feel they are not getting this.

What follows are my descriptions of some of the leading indexes you are likely to see quoted by spread betting companies. In addition to these, you may also see some proprietary sector indexes offered, based on the larger companies in each sector that the spread betting company offers. This allows you to trade particular components of the share market rather than going with an index that just provides broad-based coverage.

Because spread betting involves staking an amount of money against each point the market moves, spread betting on indexes in particular is easy to understand, including from a risk management point of view. The UK 100/FTSE 100, shown in Figure 4.1, is always being quoted on television and in the news as being up or down a given number of points. It is, therefore, easy to work out how much money you made or lost on the day. Be aware, however, that not all indexes are created equal, and that some can go up or down by more points than others.

Here we see a typical week in the life of the UK 100, or FTSE 100. As you can see, it opened the week at 5237 on 30 August (Monday 29 August was a bank holiday in the UK so the market was closed), and closed the week up 3.18% on 2 September. Overall, it does not look like the index moved

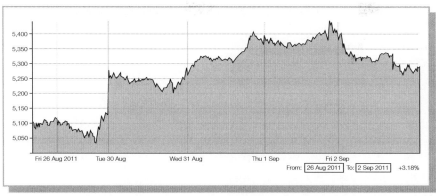

© 2011 Yahoo! Inc.

Figure 4.1   UK 100/FTSE 100: 26 August to 2 September 2011

much, but taking a look at its behaviour on a day-by-day basis, you can see there were some big moves. For example, it rose to 5237 almost immediately on the Tuesday morning (+ 108 points), and experienced a second big rally on the Wednesday, up at one stage over 120 points from the opening.

The big gap up over the weekend was the result of relief following Hurricane Irene, which narrowly missed New York. As the US regulator announced the markets in New York would open as per usual on Monday morning, traders in London were able to place buy orders, all of which hit the market when it opened on Tuesday morning.

All this relief disappeared by Friday, when poor US jobs figures were released at lunchtime, leading the market to slump on Friday afternoon.

As you can see, a beginner betting £1 per point on the UK 100 index would not have suffered many large and nasty losses on this average week (someone with a long FTSE 100 bet on for Friday at £1 per point would have lost just over £100).

It also shows that the index was able to range through a high of 5442 to a low of 5036. Worst case scenario, someone who was extremely unlucky, who went short the index at £1/point at 5036 and exited at 5442, would have lost just over £400.

Now, let's look at the Nikkei 225 (Japan 225) for the same week.

Here we see the Nikkei opened the week at 8779 and closed it at 8950. The difference in points looks small, but look how much activity there was in this index during the week. More importantly, think in terms here of the spread bet at even £1/point. The Nikkei, at over 9000 points, is a bigger market than the FTSE, and consequently capable of moving further during the trading day than the FTSE. It is crucial that the beginning trader, even when experimenting with indexes, understands how some indexes can be more profitable – and more dangerous – than others.

There are some big moves here, like the big leap from 8850 to around 8970, or the similar gap upwards on the Thursday morning Japanese time. The Tuesday morning advance was prompted partly by relief that Hurricane Irene did not do more damage to New York, while on the Thursday morning positive manufacturing figures from China did much to lift the index and buoy the moods of traders in Tokyo.

At the end of the week, we see another big gap in the morning, this time downwards. The poor US jobs report which emerged on the Friday did not hit the Japanese market because it had already closed. The announcement that Japan had a new finance minister made little impact. Traders were more concerned about the reports that domestic Japanese manufacturers had cut their capital spending, and that the stronger yen was hitting the operating profits of big electronics manufacturers like Sony.

For the spread bettor, there were several big gaps in this market during the week of 50–100 points, offering potential for both profits and losses. They tend to occur in the morning on this chart, as the Japanese market has had time to digest overnight news from Europe and the US. Smaller, but still significant moves can occur after the lunchtime break when the market in Japan shuts – there is a big gap when the lunchtime break ends

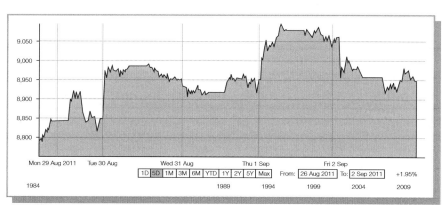

Figure 4.2   Japan 225/Nikkei 225: 29 August to 2 September 2011

on the Wednesday and a downwards move on the Friday. It is important to be aware of these sudden moves when placing stop losses as they could easily trigger a stop that is 50 points behind the price – something that is less likely in the FTSE during the same week.

Bear in mind both these charts cover a period of uncharacteristically high market volatility, and in late August, when many market participants are still on holiday, it is possible for smaller trades to have more of an impact on the market than other times in the year.

This is a valuable lesson in index trading:

1 Some indexes are bigger than others, and can move around by a greater number of points per day. When they react, they can rise or fall by a larger degree. A 100 point gain in the UK 100 is less likely than a 100 point gain in the Japan 225. There are 225 companies reporting into the Japan 225, and only 100 into the UK 100.

2 Political and economic news, even if it breaks in a different country – in this case it was a US government announcement – can still have an impact on indexes. Here we have stock markets in Japan and the UK reacting to the slow-down in US manufacturing growth and job numbers.

3 Overnight news can cause sudden market reactions as soon as the market opens. You can see in Figures 4.1 and 4.2 that both indexes experience some of their biggest moves as soon as trading begins and overnight orders are placed. As a spread bettor, it is very hard to benefit from all this price action, unless you had an open bet on the index already. Spread betting companies will seek to open a bet for you as soon as they can, but at times when markets are gapping up like this, it can be difficult for dealers, and even automated trading systems, to open bets immediately.

Spread betting versus exchange traded funds (ETFs)

Stock market indexes have long been used as the basis for investment products of one type or another. In particular, they have underpinned the recent and spectacular growth in exchange traded funds (ETFs). These are funds that seek to track an index as closely as possible, by purchasing shares in the same proportion as the index. The idea here is that they are passively managed – i.e. there is no active investment management going on, the ETF will just seek to duplicate the performance of the index as closely as possible – and therefore the fees charged by the fund can be a lot lower.

The other advantage is that the ETF is listed like a share on a recognised stock exchange, and can be bought and sold like a share, making these products more accessible to investors. Because they track indexes, they can be treated as a proxy for owning the market.

Spread betting indexes does, however, offer some advantages over ETFs, at least for short-term trading. You have a very similar selection of indexes at your fingertips, and can buy and sell them just as easily. You don't own a physical asset, however; this is still just a bet. In addition, a spread bet is not something you can readily include in your ISA or pension portfolio, nor would you want to, while many pension funds now invest in ETFs.

Spread bets and ETFs also share some characteristics: ETFs charge their owners management fees, while spread bets cost traders via the spread. ETFs will start to deviate from the index they track (it is very difficult to exactly replicate the performance of an index, even if you hold all the appropriate shares in exactly the right ratios – there are still the brokerage costs incurred as you re-balance every month), while spread bets bring with them over-night financing costs and the roll-over costs at contract expiry time.

Popular indexes used for spread betting

UK 100 (FTSE 100)

The FTSE 100 index is the most widely followed UK stock market index. It comprises the top 100 UK listed companies, ranked by market capitalisation. Together, they account for more than 80 per cent of the value of all the companies listed on the London Stock Exchange. It is sometimes referred to as the UK 100 by financial spread betting and CFD trading companies.

The FTSE 100 does not, however, provide comprehensive exposure to companies with a strong UK bias, as many large international corporations are included in the index. Typical examples at the time of writing include HSBC (global banking giant), Royal Dutch Shell (Netherlands oil company), Xstrata (Australian miner) and Antofagasta (Chilean miner).

Many foreign or global companies like to list in London as this helps them to raise capital via a UK share issue. In effect, the FTSE 100 reflects the prices of the largest companies listed in London, regardless of nationality. The index uses a free float methodology to determine the impact of individual share prices on the daily performance of the index. This means only shares

Table 4.2 Spread bets versus exchange traded funds (ETFs)

Spread bets	ETFs
Tax free in UK and Ireland	Subject to capital gains tax unless held in ISA
Over-The-Counter (OTC) derivative with price quoted by broker	Listed on regulated exchange
Financing charge for trades outside one day	Custody fees from broker as per shares
Margin trading	Bought and sold in physical share market, some ETFs make use of very limited leverage
Based on futures prices	Can be based on either futures or physical asset prices
Trade commodities and currencies	Can trade commodities, currencies becoming available gradually
Not suitable for long-term trading due to financing costs	Cheaper to hold long term, but futures rollover can cause deviation from spot price after 3–6 months
No management fee	Small management charge from ETF provider
Used by retail investors	Used by retail and institutional investors
Short markets	Some ETFs can short specific markets (inverse performance)

that are being traded freely count towards the capitalisation figure, not shares held by insiders or other strategic shareholdings.

The components of the index are reviewed every quarter. Companies in the FTSE 250 index, which have reached a capitalisation that would place them in the top 90 companies in the FTSE 100, are promoted into the index. At the time of writing, the largest four companies in the index were HSBC, Royal Dutch Shell, Vodafone Group and GlaxoSmithKline.

The index opens at 08.00 UK time, and closes at 16.30. Some spread betting companies will continue to quote prices on this index both in advance of the opening time and after closing time, as there are also futures contracts available to trade outside normal trading hours. It is best to check with your broker to see what the trading times for the UK 100 index are. It may not be the same as the actual London Stock Exchange trading hours.

The US 30 (Dow Jones Industrial Average)

The Dow Jones Industrial Average (DJIA) is one of the most famous financial markets indexes in the world. Launched in 1896, it tracks the average price of the largest 30 stocks traded in the United States. These days it does not just include industrial companies, but a wide range of American corporate titans.

The Dow is still widely used as a public measure of the performance of the US share market, although many professional money managers now consider the Standard & Poor's (S&P) 500 to be a better representation. The Dow is often referred to as the US 30 by financial spread betting and CFD trading companies.

This index is price weighted, which means that each share makes up a proportion of the index based on its price. The more expensive the share price, the bigger the role it is going to play in the way the index behaves. Because of this, the Dow does not necessarily reflect the underlying market value of the companies: a company which issues more shares may be more valuable as a whole, but its share price could be lower than a smaller company that issues fewer shares.

However, because of stock splits and other adjustments to the shares of the major companies that make up the Dow, the index is calculated using the *Dow divisor*, a re-balancing method that ensures that if there is a sudden change in the value of a share price due to a corporate action like a stock split, the value of the index in points does not change. Otherwise, a stock split might drive down the value of the index, while the fundamental value of the underlying companies in the market has not changed at all!

It is also important to note that the Dow components are not just companies listed on the New York Stock Exchange. These days there are NASDAQ (National Association of Securities Dealers Automated Quotations) companies included as well. Ultimately, if you are trading a spread bet based on the Dow, you are betting on the aggregated price of the 30 largest listed companies in America.

The US 500 (S&P 500)

The Standard & Poor's 500 is considered the best single gauge of the US equities market, better even than its more famous cousin, the Dow Jones Industrial Average. This is because it tracks a broader number of US companies' shares. It follows the bigger, more liquid US shares, companies with a market capitalisation of more than $3 billion.

The index is maintained by Standard & Poor's, which calculates its official prices and works out which companies will compose the index. All the companies in the index must be real companies; closed ended funds, holding companies and partnerships are excluded. In addition, over 50 per cent of the shares in the company must be available to be traded in the open market, also known as the 'public float'.

The S&P 500 is younger than the Dow, having been launched in the 1950s. Its size reflects the much larger number of US listed companies that were available to trade by the 1950s. The composition of the index is determined by the S&P index committee, which follows a set of published guidelines that lay down which companies should be included, and which excluded. The committee seeks to ensure that the index reflects a balanced range of business sectors, and that the companies tracked are actively traded. This aids in the replication of the index by portfolio managers, tracker funds and others.

Nikkei 225 (Japan 225)

The Nikkei 225 index, often quoted as the Japan 225 by online trading companies, is widely regarded as the benchmark stock market index for the Tokyo Stock Exchange. It is calculated on a daily basis by the *Nihon Keizai Shimbun* (*Nikkei*), a Japanese business newspaper. It has been published regularly since 1950, and since January 2010 it has been updated every 15 seconds during trading sessions.

The Japan/Nikkei 225 is the most popular Asian index among traders. Although the index has never returned to the heights it achieved in the final stages of the Japanese 'bubble' economy in 1989, it represents a market that is highly liquid and quite efficient.

Like the Dow Jones Industrial Average, the Nikkei 225 is price weighted, meaning the more expensive the share price, the more weight is attached to that company in the index. The index constituents are considered to be the largest and most actively traded companies listed in Tokyo. Because the index is meant to reflect the whole market, albeit roughly, there are no enforced sector weightings. The annual review of the index takes place in September and takes effect from the beginning of October.

Germany 30 (DAX)

The DAX index (Deutsche AktienIndeX), also widely known as the Germany 30 by online trading companies, is the benchmark stock market index for Germany. It is the main indicator for the performance of the price of major German listed companies on the Frankfurt Stock Exchange, and represents about 80 per cent of the total market value of German shares.

To be included in the index, apart from its market capitalisation, a company usually has to have been trading for three years, with at least 15 per cent of its value represented by actively traded shares, and it must also be deriving sufficient revenues from within Germany to be considered representative of the German economy.

The price of the index is calculated using the Xetra electronic trading system on a second-by-second basis. The component companies are determined by their order book volume and market capitalisation. The index is re-balanced on a quarterly basis.

The DAX was launched on 30 December 1987, using a starting price of 1,000. Among the companies included in the DAX are globally recognised names such as Adidas, BMW, Lufthansa, Merck and Siemens.

Europe 50 (Eurostoxx 50)

The Eurostoxx 50 index was created to track the share prices of the largest 50 blue chip companies in the Eurozone. With the creation of the Eurozone, it was felt that a stock market index was needed that could represent the fortunes of the largest listed companies among the 12 countries in the euro. The Eurostoxx 50 captures 60 per cent of the total 'free float' market capitalisation of the Eurozone's listed companies, namely the bulk of the publicly available and regularly traded shares.

While the DAX and CAC index are widely followed by traders interested in European markets, the Eurostoxx represents a better pan-regional measure of the performance of the most liquid and largest European stocks. Its cousin, the Eurostoxx Total Market Index (TMI) covers 95 per cent of the Eurozone's share market.

The Eurostoxx 50 provides exposure to some large companies that are not traded in either Paris or Frankfurt, including the likes of Aegon (Netherlands), Arcelor Mittal (Luxembourg), BBVA (Spain) and Nokia (Finland). The index, designed by Stoxx, a company owned by Deutsche Boerse, the main equities exchange in Germany, is the most widely recognised blue chip stock market benchmark for the Eurozone.

UK 250 (FTSE 250)

The FTSE 250 index, often referred to as the UK 250 by spread betting firms, is a stock market index which tracks the largest 250 companies listed on the London Stock Exchange, after those in the FTSE 100. While the FTSE 100 represents the largest companies with shares traded in London, the 250 includes the group below the FTSE 100.

Many fund managers and investors feel the FTSE 250 is a better indicator of the performance of the UK market than the FTSE 100 (or UK 100), because more of the companies included in it derive the bulk of their revenues from business done in the UK. The latter is composed of a much higher proportion of multi-nationals or large foreign firms that have chosen to list in London for capital raising purposes.

The FTSE 250 is a capitalisation weighted index: this means that companies are included based on the size of their market capitalisation, the value of the shares they have out there in the market. The index also contains a large number of investment trusts. These are investment vehicles which issue shares on the stock market. They are managed like mutual funds, but investors buy into them by acquiring shares. At the time of writing, JPMorgan alone had six of its investment trusts as constituents of the FTSE 350 (the FTSE 100 and FTSE 250 combined).

Like the FTSE 100, the FTSE 250 has several foreign firms or multi-nationals with substantial interests outside the UK. It also frequently trades very closely (correlates) with the FTSE 100.

Tech 100/Technology 100/US Tech 100 (NASDAQ)

The NASDAQ, launched in the USA in 1971, was the first electronic securities exchange, and remains the largest electronic equities trading market in the world. The NASDAQ 100 index represents the 100 largest non-financial NASDAQ listed stocks by market capitalisation. You will usually see it quoted as a spread bet using some combination of the words 'Tech' or 'Technology' and the number '100'. Don't confuse it with the TechDAX, however, which is a German index that tracks the 30 largest technology companies listed in Frankfurt, and can also sometimes be quoted as a spread bet.

During the infamous 'dot com' boom in 1999–2000, the NASDAQ was followed particularly closely as many of the new economy companies such as Amazon and Google, as well as hardware manufacturers like Dell and Intel, are included in the NASDAQ 100.

The index is re-adjusted on a quarterly basis, but the emphasis is on reflecting the economic importance of the constituent companies, many of which are large corporations in the fields of technology, bio-science and retail.

The index has a reputation for being heavily laced with technology companies and firms which have grown up recently, rather than the more established shares investors will find on the New York Stock Exchange, hence its ongoing association with the technology sector. Among the big names in the index can be found Apple, Cisco Systems, Genzyme and Yahoo!, as well as non-technology game changers such as Starbucks.

Spread betting on share prices

A wide range of shares, particularly UK shares, are now readily available to spread bet on. The number varies depending on the spread betting company with which you are dealing. Some spread betting companies offer prices on literally thousands of shares, although you will not necessarily see all these on your trading screen. It is worth checking by phoning the firm and asking them if they can quote you a price, as often they will be able to.

Most companies will offer prices on all the companies in all the major stock market indexes (often referred to as the index components). These will be the largest and most liquid companies around the world, with a high daily volume of trades in the real market. A good spread betting company should be able to quote prices on all the companies in the FTSE 350 index.

It is possible to spread bet on smaller companies as well, but you will generally find that the smaller you go in the market, the wider the spread and the higher the margin rate (I have seen 50 per cent margin quoted on some UK smaller companies).

The attraction of smaller companies to some traders is the fact that their price can change very quickly, and with the added leverage obtained from margin trading, they hope to augment their profits. This is particularly the case in the energy sector, where news of finds by energy exploration companies can rapidly change their share price. Be warned, however, as with all trading, what goes up can also go down just as quickly. Prices in smaller companies can fall rapidly overnight, and you can find your stops triggered and your trade closed out at well below the price you had set as your stop loss price.

Remember, spread bets are not real shares, so you won't get any share certificates, voting rights or any of the other perks associated with holding physical shares. A spread bet is just an agreement, a contract between you and the spread betting company.

Treatment of dividends

When trading shares in the real world, as an investor you will benefit from the payment of dividends on your shares. In the world of spread betting, because you don't really own a share in that company, you won't benefit from the dividend. However, the share price of a company tends to drop immediately after the dividend date, as the dividend has been paid, and another won't be along for another three to six months at least. This drop in price will tend to match the value of the dividend that has just been paid out, which is great if you were a shareholder, but not so great if you were a spread bettor.

In order to compensate their customers who are long the stock when the dividend is paid out, spread betting companies will credit them with the dividend yield based on their total exposure to that company at the time the dividend is paid. This way they don't need to worry about taking a hit from the fall in the company's share price as the share goes ex-dividend. It is still worth knowing when this is going to happen, because while your cash position might be credited, the price will still fall, and you will feel foolish if it breaks through your stop loss.

If, on the other hand, you are short at the time the dividend is paid, you will be debited the dividend yield. This might seem unfair on the surface, but it stops everyone from going short on shares that are just about to go ex-dividend. Be aware, therefore, of the dividend dates of companies you are shorting. If they are in real trouble, of course, the dividend they pay out will be minimal, and you won't have to worry, but it is still worth thinking about if you plan on aggressively shorting a company.

Other corporate actions

There are a number of other important events beyond dividends that can affect the fortunes of a share price in the real market. These include rights issues, stock splits and the suspension of trading of a share (called 'corporate actions').

In the case of a rights issue, when a company seeks to raise more money by issuing more shares, usually offered at a discount to its existing shareholders first, the price of the existing shares in the market is likely to go down. There are more shares out there, and unless the company is one of the most highly sought after investments in the history of capitalism, its share price will probably give up some ground. For the spread bettor, a rights issue is only going to affect the price. You will not be offered a larger position size by your spread betting company; indeed many of your fellow traders may be taking up short positions to benefit from the fall in the share price, forcing the spread betting company to hedge its risk.

What happens if a company goes to the wall, or its shares are suspended, while you have an open spread bet? Policies differ between the spread betting companies, so it is worth exploring this before it happens.

Often, the spread betting company will simply freeze the trade until there is some form of resolution. This can take quite some time, for example in the case of Northern Rock. They may also ramp up the amount of margin they want you to contribute in order to keep the bet open. When Lehman Brothers collapsed, spread bettors with open bets on Lehman's share price were asked by some firms for 100 per cent margin, or their trade would be closed (i.e. the trader was asked to shoulder the entire value of the bet – the spread betting company would no longer finance it). Other companies may close the bet after a relatively short period of time, five business days for example. If the bet has an expiry date, then there is a good chance there will not be a new bet available once the current one expires.

More enterprising spread betting companies can find other ways to provide opportunities to bet on suspended shares: when Northern Rock shares were suspended in 2008, Cantor Index started running a book for its clients on the likely level of compensation that would be paid out for Northern Rock shareholders.

Remember that spread betting companies are within their rights to close bets or change margin rates and spreads whenever they like. Ultimately, they own the bet. It is in their commercial interests to be as fair as possible to you, their customer, but if changes in the underlying market force them to hike up the margin they require on a given bet, they will do so. They can even decline a bet, even though they are still quoting a price on the company.

When Bradford & Bingley shares were in trouble in 2009, some spread betting companies started to decline new short trades on B&B's share price, even though they were still quoting a price. My guess is that too many traders were going short on the shares, and the companies concerned were becoming worried about their ability to hedge out all the risk.

During the credit crisis of 2008–09, many spread bettors were asked to put up more margin at fairly short notice on some share-based bets as liquidity was draining out of the market. In some instances this could be quite dramatic, from 10 per cent up to as much as 90 per cent (and in some extreme cases all of it). This forced a lot of traders to close their positions, sometimes at a loss.

At the end of the day, if a company goes into receivership, shareholders are always the last in line to get any compensation. Spread bettors are not even in the queue. Your spread bet is an agreement between you and the spread betting company based on the price of that company; it has nothing to do with ownership of the company. It does not confer a stake to you, but is instead governed by the terms and conditions of the spread betting company with which you are trading.

Hedging shares with spread bets

A spread bet can also be used as a tool to hedge shares in the real market. If you have substantial investments, say in a tracker product or perhaps in shares in the FTSE 100 index, and you turn bearish on the market, one option might be to sell those shares, go to cash, and buy them back later when they are cheaper.

However, in doing so you can incur a range of costs, including not only the broker commissions you pay for selling your shares and buying them back later, but also capital gains tax and stamp duty on top of this if you hold them outside your ISA (Individual Savings Account).

A spread bet can be a cost-effective way to minimise losses from a share portfolio, because it can allow you to go short on the market. By opening a short trade based on your physical shares, you can make money to off-set the losses you might sustain if your negative views turn out to be correct.

A simple example would be a FTSE 100 tracker product, possibly an ISA. With £5,000 in an ISA, and the notion that the FTSE might be in for a correction, you decide to open a short spread bet. But how big should your trade be?

With the FTSE being quoted at 5764/5767 to sell, divide your total FTSE exposure (£5,000) by its current level (say 5766) to get 0.867. It would be difficult to get a spread betting company to take an 86 pence per point bet, but £1/point would give you some decent short side exposure for a £5,000 portfolio. If you had a £10,000 portfolio, you might be looking to hedge at £2/point. Some spread betting companies take smaller minimum trade sizes. At time of writing, the likes of ETX Capital, IG Index and Finspreads were offering less than £1 a point on some markets. If the market fell, as you expected, then while you were losing money in the real market, you would be making money in the spread betting market.

Let's say the FTSE lost 100 points over the course of the week after you opened your spread bet.

Loss to portfolio: £86

Spread bet gain @ £1/point: £100 (minus the spread, usually around £1–£3 depending on your provider)

You made slightly more money than you lost, largely because you were taking on slightly more risk. Had the spread betting company been able to quote you 86 pence per point, you'd have been able to neutralise your loss.

If the market had turned the other way, and had risen 100 points, against your expectations, your hedge would have ended up at:

Gain to portfolio: £86

Spread bet loss @ £1/point: £100

In this case, you are out of pocket to the tune of £14, a much smaller price to pay than the £86 you would have lost.

As you can see, spread betting makes more sense as a hedging tool to protect larger portfolios, to the tune of £20,000 and up. If you are holding a number of FTSE 100 shares, it would still make sense to use a UK 100 short bet to hedge them if you felt the market as a whole was heading for a rocky patch.

It is also possible to hedge your risk in a single share, particularly a larger company. The principle is the same. A single share is a bigger risk too, and liable to sustain a more sudden price change than the FTSE 100 index.

Example

Hedging BP shares after Deepwater Horizon

Here's an example of someone who is holding £10,000 of British Petroleum shares at the time of the Deepwater Horizon blow-out in April 2010. At the time of the fateful explosion on BP's Gulf of Mexico rig, the company's share price was trading at around 630 to 640 pence. As it became obvious that the oil company was not going to be able to stop the oil leaking from the well immediately, and the ugly spectre of litigation raised its head, the share price began to fall as more investors unloaded stock.

At this stage, there was still a lot of rumour and uncertainty surrounding the evolving situation in the Gulf of Mexico. Rather than sell his shares, our hypothetical investor decides to hedge the whole value. Looking at his spread betting account the week after the blow-out, he sees:

BP offer @ 600p

How big a bet does he need to take out to make sure he is 100 per cent hedged? With the share price at around the 600 pence mark (he is expecting it will continue to fall), to hedge £10,000 of BP he would need to be betting against BP at £16 per point (his exposure *per pence* in BP is £16.70 – to hedge it, he would need to bet either £16 or £17 per point, or £16.50 if he can get it).

Assuming the price of BP shares fell to 400 pence per share (it actually fell even further), a loss of 200 pence, while our investor would have lost £3,340 on his shares, his spread bet would make him £3,200.

Assuming that BP was quoted at 3 per cent margin (typical for a share of this kind), he would still need to commit £288 of his trading capital to finance his spread bet (16 × 600 /100 × 3 = 288).

Hedging of this nature is not really a short-term strategy. It is a way of protecting your longer-term investments at times when you think their value might be harmed. You can close your short trades once you feel the market is recovering. Efficient hedging requires that you calculate accurately how much you need to hedge in order to protect your original investments. Some investors do not feel the need to protect their entire long portfolio, but like to feel they can off-set some of their losses with a short position.

Can I hold spread bets in my ISA or pension?

At the time of writing, there have been some early efforts to look at the scope for holding spread bets in an Individual Savings Account or Self-Invested Personal Pensions (SIPPs), but no companies currently offer these and I would be surprised if they ever do. For instance, an ISA is already tax free, so while spread betting makes more sense if you have already exhausted your annual ISA tax free allowance, it does not make sense for a tax free spread bet to be contained in the tax free ISA wrapper.

Spread bets are short-term trading instruments with no rights of owner-ship over anything. In addition, they bring with them a hefty burden of leverage via the margin trading mechanism. What makes them suitable for longer-term investing or for a pension scheme is anyone's guess, but I personally cannot see the advantages. This has not stopped some spread betting companies from looking at whether this would be possible. I would be surprised, however, if the UK regulator ever approves spread bets for ISAs or SIPPs. There are sensible ways to complement these investment schemes with spread bets, but they are not, and never should be, considered as solid and stable long-term investments.

5

Commodities for the first timer

Financial spread betting is now one of the most cost-effective ways to trade global commodities markets. Perhaps the most high profile and widely traded commodities for spread bets are oil and gold. However, with the ongoing boom in commodities prices, more traders are looking at other markets, including favourites like copper and silver.

As ever with spread betting, you are not trading the actual physical commodity markets, nor are you trading commodities futures contracts. You are trading a price quoted by your spread betting company, which will be loosely based on the underlying commodities futures market. Even so, as a private investor, spread betting remains the most effective way to capitalise on the large trends we have seen materialising in commodities markets in the last few years.

What drives commodities markets?

If you're considering focusing your trading activities in the field of commodities – and many traders do – you need to be aware of the specific dynamics that drive these markets. Prices for commodities are driven by the balance between supply and demand. Demand for commodities depends on the overall economic health of countries that are big consumers such as the US, China, Germany and Japan. Each country releases monthly data on the growth of its gross domestic product (GDP), industrial manufacturing and employment levels and these provide a good general picture about which way global demand is moving.

If, for instance, data in the US shows that unemployment is rising, this means that Americans will have less disposable income to spend on cars, television sets, houses or luxuries, which in turn will translate into lower demand for oil, copper, gold and coffee.

Developing countries in Asia play an increasingly important role in global commodities demand, particularly for industrial commodities, such as metals, and those that have more of an investment-type nature, such as gold and silver. It is therefore useful to keep an eye on economic indicators from India, Brazil, Russia and, most importantly, China.

On the supply side, each commodity has its own supply chain and the trade associations that represent the producers of specific types of commodity typically publish monthly or quarterly data about supply levels. Any indication of oversupply or a slow-down in demand will be an indicator that prices are about to start declining.

Unlike shares, commodities have a cyclical quality and over a longer period of time tend to repeat something that resembles a boom and bust cycle. If a company is in trouble, a share price can, in theory, fall until it reaches zero (although mostly share trading either grinds to a halt before that or is suspended). Commodities, however, have a cut-off point and that point is cost of production. If, for argument's sake, it costs $500 to produce a tonne of copper, then if prices were to fall below this level, producers would stop production because they would start losing money.

What happens in real life is that the average producer mines copper at a theoretical $500/tonne, while a small number of producers mine copper at a higher price. This can either be because their technology costs more or because they are mining an ore that is less rich. The cost of the most expensive copper is called the marginal cost of production and, if prices start falling, such producers are the first to have to stop mining, thus reducing copper supplies in the market and leading to a re-balancing of prices. This is universal across all commodities markets; if prices become too low, a certain amount of production is wiped out of the market.

When it comes to agricultural commodities such as wheat, corn or soybeans, farmers will frequently switch from the cheapest crop to the most expensive. It takes about three months for metals producers to react to very low prices and about six months for farmers to adjust their production.

Oil, one of the most popular spread betting markets, is governed by a slightly different dynamic. Here, the producer cartel OPEC (Organization of Petroleum Exporting Countries) will decide on the levels each of its 11 member countries will export over a future period depending on world prices. OPEC's aim is to maintain a balanced price that is profitable for producers without being prohibitively expensive for their buyers, who will start looking for substitutes if they feel that prices have remained too high for too long. That, at least, is the theory, and in the past OPEC members have ignored their own agreements and pumped more oil in order for the countries in question to keep earning.

Gold is the only commodity that defies the logic of simple physical demand and supply because, on top of the demand for the actual metal in the form of jewellery and bars, it is also seen as a safe-haven investment, an alternative currency and a store of value. Most economic situations are good for gold because they result in at least one of the group of buyers of the precious metal increasing demand.

Who buys commodities?

Over the past decade, commodities have become increasingly popular with large investors such as pension funds and insurance companies. These institutional investors had only limited exposure to commodities in the past, because commodities were perceived as a risky investment – investments in futures and options are highly leveraged. The risk has not gone down over the years, but the tolerance towards speculative investment seems to have risen.

The two most frequently traded commodities are oil and gold, but other commodities such as base metals, precious metals and agricultural commodities have become more popular in recent years. Oil is the top energy commodity, and other commodities in the same group include natural gas, gasoline, heating oil and power. The two trading hubs are the New York Mercantile Exchange (NYMEX) in New York and the Intercontinental Exchange (ICE) in London.

Copper and aluminium are the most widely traded base metals while nickel, zinc, tin and lead attract far smaller volumes of trade. The London Metal Exchange, the world's biggest and oldest metal futures exchange, has added a steel futures contract in the last few years, but as with all new contracts, it takes time for it to become established and, to my knowledge, it is not currently available as a spread betting market.

Alongside gold, other precious metals include silver, platinum and palladium. Futures for all the metals are traded in New York, while over-the-counter metals are traded in London and Switzerland, a major precious metals hub.

Agriculture covers the widest group of commodities and is broken down into grains; wheat, corn, soybean and rice; soft commodities like cocoa, sugar and coffee; livestock such as cattle, feeder cattle, live hogs and pork bellies, and those that don't fall into any particular group such as orange juice and cotton. Most of these markets are now available via a spread betting account.

Spread betting on agricultural commodities

With a finite amount of land available for farming, farmers will switch between crops depending on which one pays the most. For instance, a drive to be energy independent has led the United States to stimulate domestic production of biofuels in recent years, a move which has caused farmers to plant large swathes of the country's grain belt with corn instead of soybeans or wheat. In Brazil, the world's largest producer of coffee and sugar, sugar is the preferred raw material for making bioethanol.

All the agricultural commodities depend heavily on the weather and some will only grow in a specific climate. Oranges are partial to a warm climate, while cocoa will only thrive in a rain-forest type of environment. Grains are the most geographically diverse, but require the right amount of rain at crucial times of growth and relatively dry weather for the harvest. Droughts or excessive rainfall can devastate a year's crop and will cause temporary spikes in prices. Harvests are the periods of lowest prices and in the case of grains, which are grown around the globe, those harvests come at different times of the year. As with livestock, plant diseases can decimate a crop and lead to price spikes.

The US Department of Agriculture (USDA) provides extensive information on all agricultural commodities, while a number of websites track the weather across the globe.

The main spread betting commodities markets

While many investors come to spread betting with at least a passing familiarity with shares and the FTSE index, far fewer really understand the commodities markets. Gold and crude oil are tracked on a regular basis in the business press these days, but other commodities markets are only touched upon on occasion. Having said that, coverage of commodities has increased in size and quality in the media over the last few years, as commodities have left other asset classes, such as equities, in their dust.

Trading commodities can be risky. It is possible to identify significant trends in commodities markets using technical analysis, but be aware that some commodities markets see more volume – and thus are often priced more efficiently – than others. Those traders who have been able to profit consistently in commodities markets, in my experience, have shared a couple of characteristics above and beyond the generic qualities shared by all successful traders:

1 They focus on only one or two markets: great commodities traders earn their salt from just following one market, maybe two. The second, junior market may be something they trade when the senior market is looking quiet, with little price action.

2 They know their market inside out. This goes beyond simply looking at charts. They understand the dynamics of the market, who the producers are, who the consumers are, what the seasonal and political factors are. They can often be boring dinner party guests, as they spout forth on the merits of the rival gas pipelines in eastern Europe, or industrial usage of platinum, but this is what gives them their edge – they do their homework, they know their price history and they can see the news behind the news.

Big commodities traders are resourceful: part of their success is their ability to voraciously hoover up information on their market. I've seen them looking at satellite photographs of the American Midwest to try to gauge the quality of the new wheat harvest, or employing researchers in West Africa to patrol coffee plantations and interview farmers. I'm not suggesting the average spread bettor will be able to command the resources of a commodities hedge fund, but this should illustrate that there is no replacement for homework in commodities (other than, perhaps, amazing luck).

Below are some of the most popular commodities markets for spread betting clients. I have included a fair amount of background information on each to serve as a primer for the novice commodities trader. This should help guide you towards the information sources you may want to research further, as well as perhaps giving you an initial feel for each market. From this you should be able to form an idea about the commodities markets that interest you.

Crude oil

Crude oil is the world's most heavily traded commodity. The volumes of trade in oil that flow daily through commodities exchanges dwarf those for other commodities. This is because buyers and sellers in the market include not only speculators, funds and investors but also oil producers and refiners who use futures to hedge their exposure, that is, cushion themselves from price swings by fixing prices three, six, twelve months or even longer in advance. This has led to an efficient market, and is why you will usually find the narrowest spreads are for crude oil on the commodities section of your spread betting platform.

Oil futures are traded on New York Mercantile Exchange (NYMEX), which is the most liquid market for oil futures; the Intercontinental Exchange (ICE), the key oil exchange in Europe; the Shanghai Futures Exchange (SHFE) and the Tokyo Commodities Exchange (TOCOM).

West Texas Intermediate (WTI) is the most popular futures contract traded on NYMEX with 170 million lots traded in 2010. Until recently WTI was considered the benchmark contract for the oil industry, but in recent years the price for WTI has dropped, even at times when oil supplies around the globe have been tight, because WTI reflects the regional US storage and transportation dynamic rather than that of the rest of the world. WTI's nearest rival, Brent Crude oil, a type of oil from the North Sea traded on ICE in London, has risen fast and has become the key contract the industry will look at when trying to assess what the global price should be. You will often see both Brent and WTI quoted as spread bets. If a firm only quotes a 'Crude Oil' spread bet, it is worth finding out which contract it is based on, or whether it is a hybrid of the two, as this will make a big difference.

The quality of crude oil varies from field to field; it is classified according to how much sulphur it contains and how light or heavy it is. Crude oil is not used in its original form, but is refined into products such as gasoline and kerosene, a fuel for planes, and distillates such as diesel and heating oil used either to power buses, trains and machinery or to heat buildings and fire industrial boilers. The most sought-after crude oils are those called light and sweet which contain large amounts of fractions that are used to process petrol, kerosene and diesel. The term sweet comes from the practice in the early days of oil drilling when prospectors used to taste and smell a small amount of oil to determine its quality. 'Sweet' oil, or oil with low sulphur content, smells pleasant and has a mildly sweet taste.

The price of oil is a balancing act between demand and supply issues. On the supply side, oil depends on global politics more than any other commodity. Although the single largest producing country is Russia, most of the oil is produced in the Middle East and any conflicts and unrest there will be reflected in a rise in prices.

Saudi Arabia is the largest producer in OPEC. Its other key members are Algeria, Iran, Iraq, Kuwait, Libya, the United Arab Emirates, Qatar and Venezuela. OPEC ministers meet twice a year in March and September in Vienna or the Middle East to decide the levels of output in order to balance the price of oil. On the one hand, while high oil prices translate into higher income for all member states, prices can be too high, and can result in end users increasingly looking for alternatives to oil such as ethanol, a situation oil producers are keen to avoid.

Most of the oil that is pumped is used for transport, with the United States being the largest consumer in the world accounting for 22 per cent of global demand. It is closely followed by China, Japan, India and increasingly Brazil.

About half of the world's crude oil travels via tankers with global seaborne trade accounting for 42 million barrels a day in 2009. One of the weak points for oil is that, to reach its destination, it has to travel through some of the most sensitive straits and canals in the world, such as the Strait of Hormuz or the Suez Canal, which at times of political crisis such as the Arab Spring can become very vulnerable.

Apart from geopolitical news, there is a whole set of data that will move oil prices on a regular basis. The US Department of Energy's Energy Information Agency (EIA) publishes weekly levels of US oil, gasoline, diesel and heating oil inventories. Oil analysts will publish their forecasts for changes in inventory levels a day before the data release, and oil prices will move depending on how close the actual change was to the predictions. Any forecasts from OPEC ministers on predicted oil output will move prices, as will statements from the International Energy Agency (IEA), a group representing 28 key oil-consuming countries, which holds significant oil stockpiles which it very occasionally releases in order to alleviate a shortage in the market.

Natural gas

Natural gas is odourless and consists mostly of methane, the same gas that cows produce after a copious meal of grass.

It is found in the same type of geological formation as crude oil and frequently does not come on its own but as a by-product of oil extraction. In the past, if there was no way of transporting the gas – either by pipelines or in specially designed ships – it was cheaper to flare off or burn the gas at the wellheads than attempt to store it. This is still done in some African countries, but because of environmental damage the practice is becoming less and less common.

There are three distinctly different gas markets that are only loosely linked because transport of gas is dominated by pipelines and only a small portion of gas travels across the oceans. In North America, both the US and Canada are large consumers and most of the gas there travels to Henry Hub in Louisiana, which is the connection point for 13 different pipelines.

Europe is supplied by Russia, Britain, Norway and the countries of the Middle East. In the past, the world's largest producers, Russia, Qatar and Iran looked into forming the equivalent of a gas OPEC – a gas producers' cartel – with a view to controlling output and prices, but this proved unfeasible because of the long-term nature of supply contracts and because of the different political motivations of the countries in question.

Another way of transporting gas is by liquifying it, achieved by cooling it to −162°C. When liquid, gas takes up 600 times less space and can be transported in specially designed tankers that have reinforced walls designed to withstand the much higher pressure. Japan, being an island, is the biggest consumer of this type of gas and buys liquified natural gas or LNG from the US, Russia and the Middle East.

For those interested in spread betting on natural gas, the key guide price will be NYMEX natural gas futures. The futures are quoted in 10,000 million British thermal units (mmBtu) for delivery via the Sabine Pipe Line at Henry Hub in Louisiana. Natural gas futures are also traded in Europe on the Intercontinental Exchange, but turnover in 2010 was 2.1 million lots compared with 64.3 million lots on NYMEX. This means that prices are dominated by the supply and demand dynamic in the United States and the local demand there for heating and power generation.

Most of the natural gas is used for domestic and commercial heating, for power generation and in manufacturing. The highest demand for gas is therefore in the winter months and to a slightly lesser extent in the summer when it is used for cooling. Spring and autumn are typically the periods of lowest gas prices. It is worth keeping an eye on the weather in the United States as well, because extreme cold spells or a prolonged winter can boost demand and prices.

Natural gas prices have been going through a period of a slump, which was partially brought on by the fact that US producers developed shale gas technology that allows them to drill for gas horizontally rather than only vertically. This has massively increased the level of production in the US and has created a glut in the market. European countries, particularly Poland, are looking into using the same technology to increase their output of gas. Shale gas technology seems here to stay and unless there is a large new area of demand, natural gas prices could stay flat over years to come.

Gold

In the history of mankind, gold has always held a special place as an investment and a store of value, and is the closest of all commodities to being used as pure money. To this day, people turn to gold as the one form of investment that can withstand crises, wars and economic downturns.

Gold is particularly revered on the Indian subcontinent, as anybody who has been to an Indian or Pakistani wedding will attest. It is passed within a family not only as a gift but also as a form of financial insurance. The period of highest demand for gold is the fourth quarter of every year when the Indian festival season is in full swing and when gold is regularly presented as a gift. The Chinese also love gold as an investment; they do not tend to wait for special occasions but buy liberally almost regardless of market price and, at the current rate, China looks likely to overtake India as the biggest buyer of gold. In Europe, and to some degree in the United States, the preferred form of gold is bars and coins, particularly in Germany and Switzerland.

In the last decade the fastest growing form of demand for gold has been from exchange traded funds (ETFs), investment papers that trade like shares on stock exchanges and are increasingly popular with large institutional investors such as pension funds and insurance companies. Demand from ETFs keeps gold prices perpetually high, much higher than they used to be even just ten years ago. When prices rise, jewellery owners will sell gold back into the market, but this is not sufficient to off-set large buy orders from investment funds.

Another key player in the gold market is central banks, which in the past have mostly come to the market as sellers of gold aiming to raise currency or additional funds for their respective economies. More recently, however, central banks in emerging economies have become buyers of gold. Central banks hold their reserves in currencies and gold and the more world currencies fluctuate the more popular gold becomes as the choice of a reserve asset.

South Africa, China, Australia and the United States are key mining regions for gold, but the level of output has levelled out or started decreasing. In the last few years, only China has been able to increase output largely due to the opening of new mines.

Although gold prices are to some extent influenced by mining supply, political and economic factors play a much bigger role than in the case of other commodities. Geopolitical problems and economic uncertainty tend to boost gold prices as investors look for something that is considered a safe-haven investment. Gold is widely considered to be an effective hedge against inflation, and often has an inverse relationship with the dollar. So, when the dollar depreciates, demand for gold tends to increase.

The price of gold is set on futures exchanges: NYMEX in New York, the Tokyo Commodity Exchange and the Shanghai Futures Exchange. In

London, gold is traded over the counter and the price is settled in the London market in two daily gold fixes. It is negotiated between a group of market-making banks and fixed at the point at which all the members can balance their and their clients' buying and selling orders.

Copper

Copper is one of the most widely used industrial metals. The average home can contain as much as 200 kilograms of copper and an average car more than 20 kilograms of the metal in wiring, pipes, electrical appliances and components.

Copper conducts electricity extremely well, which makes it ideal for use in electrical wiring and electronics, the two industries that make up about a third of all copper demand. The construction industry accounts for another third of demand and here copper is used in pipes and roof cladding, either in the form of primary copper or mixed with zinc and tin in brass and bronze. Copper is also used in power stations and deep-sea oil platforms as it can withstand extreme environments, is non-magnetic and resistant to corrosion.

The countries that use the most copper are industrialised countries with large manufacturing bases such as the United States, large European economies, Japan, Russia and China. The price of copper is therefore closely linked to the health of the economy in these countries and economic data such as GDP, industrial production and manufacturing, which are published on a monthly basis by the respective countries, are a good indicator of the direction copper prices will be moving. Over the last decade, China has become the dominant consumer in this group and now accounts for 40 per cent of all global copper consumption.

The main mining regions for copper are Chile, Peru, China and the US, but Chile plays by far the most important role as it accounts for about 40 per cent of global exports. The largest miners in the country are state-owned Codelco and US miner Freeport McMoran, closely followed by London-listed BHP Billiton, Xtrata and Rio Tinto. A large proportion of the mines in Chile are open-pit mines, and although they are not completely safe, they are safer than traditional deep-shaft mining. Still, mining or exports can be interrupted by strikes, problems with power supplies or transport, and it is worth keeping an eye on general news from Chile, Peru and Australia, another significant producer, for events that might affect copper prices.

The prices for copper are set on three exchanges – the London Metal Exchange (LME), the Commodities Exchange (COMEX) division of NYMEX, and the Shanghai Futures Exchange (SHFE). In London, copper is traded in lots of 25 tonnes and quoted in dollars per tonne, in New York it is quoted in cents per pound and in Shanghai in renminbi per tonne.

The London Metal Exchange dominates metals trading and volumes traded in London are significantly higher than on the other two exchanges, but volumes of trading have been rising faster on COMEX than in London as some funds prefer the simpler date structure and smaller lot sizes offered in New York. Spread betting prices will tend to follow either the LME or COMEX contract.

A good indicator for demand trends is the cancelled warrant data published by the LME on a daily basis. Cancelled warrants are contracts for copper that is about to leave LME warehouses indicating demand for the metal.

Silver

The lore on silver is that it can ward off vampires and werewolves, but these days it is equally efficient as a weapon against fluctuating share prices and, like gold, a safe-haven investment. However, with prices bouncing between $4 and $40 per ounce over the course of the last decade, silver has earned the status of one of the most volatile metals.

Silver's price tends to follow that of gold, and to a slightly lesser extent that of copper, but as the market for the grey metal is much thinner than either the gold or the copper market, the link with the other two metals is occasionally broken by speculative trading. Investors interested in spread betting on silver should keep a close eye on the main producers of the metal such as London-listed Mexican miner Fresnillo, Australian mining giant BHP Billiton and Polish company KGHM PolskaMiedz. Announcements of annual production levels, mine openings and closures or mining disruptions will all have a significant effect on short-term prices.

Although people traditionally think of silver as a jewellery metal, twice as much silver is used for industrial purposes as for fashion. Silver is a component in mobile phones, medical appliances and batteries, and monthly indicators of industrial demand and manufacturing for major industrial regions such as the United States and the Eurozone countries will provide a good indication of where the market is likely to move next.

Silver futures are traded on two exchanges in the US, on the COMEX division of NYMEX and the Chicago Board of Trade (CBOT). COMEX still holds the upper hand in terms of volume of trade, although the difference between the two exchanges has become academic since both were acquired by the Chicago Mercantile Group (CME Group). In terms of trading, the main difference is that although both exchanges offer a standard futures contract of 5,000 troy ounces quoted in dollars, COMEX also trades a mini silver contract of 2,500 troy ounces, while CBOT has gone even smaller with a contract size of 1,000 troy ounces.

In the case of both exchanges, it is possible to trade the contract up to 60 months ahead. London also has a thriving silver market, but here the silver is traded over-the-counter, that is, as physical metal rather than futures.

The daily price is settled by a group of market-making banks in what is called the London silver fixing. The fix begins at 12.15 p.m. and is a negotiation between members; the price is fixed at the point at which all the members can balance their and their clients' buying and selling orders.

The daily pulse of the silver market can be taken by looking at the COMEX inventories and contract open interest – the total number of outstanding contracts held by futures markets participants at the end of each day. Longer-term data such as demand and supply statistics is provided by the Silver Institute, a miners' association based in Washington.

Platinum

Platinum is the rarest speculatively traded precious metal. Even in the most platinum rich mines of South Africa, it can take between 15 and 20 tonnes of raw ore to produce just one ounce of this pale-coloured metal. It is the single most expensive commodity traded on world exchanges. A tonne of copper cost about $10,000 in 2010. In comparison, to buy a tonne of platinum in the same year would have cost about $64 million.

Most people associate platinum with elegant jewellery, and certainly among buyers of luxury goods it has replaced gold as the most covetable of metals. However, although one-third of all platinum is indeed used for luxury items, the greatest demand for the precious metal comes from the car industry. Here it is built into catalytic converters to reduce the amount of emissions from car exhausts. Ever more stringent emissions regulation in both Europe and the United States has resulted in new cars produced in the Western world having to be fitted with catalytic converters to cut down the amount of carbon dioxide released during driving. Researchers have experimented with silver, palladium and other cheaper alternatives to platinum, but the metal has proved by far the most efficient in reducing car emissions. This has not only pushed the price of platinum sky high, but will also ensure steady platinum demand for years to come.

Most of the world's platinum comes from the deep mines in South Africa, where a small group of companies including Anglo Platinum, Impala and Lonmin produce over three-quarters of the world's supply. South African mines are deeper than any others in the world and in some cases it can take a full 24 hours to travel to the furthest end of a platinum mine.

After South Africa, Russia is the largest producer and recently Zimbabwe has nudged into third place on the world scene. This concentration of production in one area of the world has created problems and in the past South Africa has grappled with strikes, inconsistent electricity supplies and mining disasters that have interrupted the supply of platinum onto the world markets. When this happens, prices start moving higher fairly quickly. It is not easy to make up for lost production with new mining, but any continued period of very high prices starts attracting scrap platinum into the market in the form of second-hand jewellery and used metal from old cars and electronic goods.

Over the last few years the balance of supply and demand has moved in favour of demand because of the increasing popularity of ETFs. Although platinum ETFs are financial paper, they have to be backed up by an amount of the actual physical platinum as well.

The two main trading centres for platinum are London, where it is traded over-the-counter, and New York, where it is traded in the form of futures and options. Good sources of statistics are UK-based precious metals company Johnson Matthey, which publishes bi-annual reviews on production and supply levels of platinum, and consultancy GFMS, which publishes an annual survey of all the precious metals markets.

Given its dependence on the car industry, car sales statistics are also a good indicator of the trend for platinum demand. The US publishes statistics on its car sales at the beginning of the month while European car sales data are released on the 15th of each month.

Coffee

The aromatic coffee bean, which helps get the world going in the morning, is bought and sold by roasters, investors and speculators on commodities exchanges across the globe. Two main types of bean dominate trade; the smoother and more expensive Arabica and, as the name suggests, the more robustly flavoured Robusta coffee. Like gems, coffee beans are graded based on the level of imperfection they carry; grade 1 is of the highest quality with minimal faults, while grade 5 is the lowest quality coffee. The benchmark price for coffee is set at commodity exchanges; for instance, grade 3 washed Arabica beans are traded on the New York Mercantile Exchange and all the other grades are priced either at a premium or a discount to that price. Robusta coffee is traded on ICE in London.

The coffee tree is a sensitive plant and likes only warm climates without frost, which would explain why all 53 countries in which coffee is grown are located near the equator. Brazil is by far the biggest producer, followed by Vietnam, Indonesia and Columbia. Arabica grows mostly in Latin America and East Africa while southeast Asia is the home of Robusta.

It takes three to five years for a coffee tree to reach maturity and a fully mature tree will produce about a pound of packaged coffee per year. At harvest time the green beans are traditionally hand-picked, although coffee farmers are increasingly moving towards strip picking, leading to a total harvest of some 7 million tonnes of green coffee beans per year.

Coffee prices on the world markets depend on steady supplies; weather extremes like frosts in producing countries, pests and diseases can reduce supplies and cause prices to move higher. The International Coffee Organization, an association of coffee producing countries, is a good source of statistics and information on coffee production levels.

Cocoa

Cocoa is the powder ground from the seeds of the cocoa or cacao tree. The tree's botanical name is *Theobroma cocoa*, which stands for 'the food of Gods', something that will not come as a surprise to chocolate lovers the world over.

A cocoa tree looks a little like an apple tree but with broader leaves. Each tree produces between 20–30 pods a year and it takes a whole year's crop from one tree to make one pound of cocoa. Cocoa is a capricious plant that likes the heat and damp and will only grow within 10 degrees north or south of the equator in rain-forest type conditions. The Ivory Coast, Ghana and Indonesia produce two-thirds of the world's cocoa and of the three countries, the Ivory Coast is by far the most significant producer.

In 2002, Ivory Coast was split by a coup into the government-controlled south and rebel-controlled north, and conflict has persisted ever since.

Throughout the decade, the country continued exporting cocoa, but the political situation there remains precarious, with exports banned in the past for political reasons. When this happens, Ghana usually steps in with increased production to alleviate some of the shortfall.

Apart from politics, weather and disease play a major role in how much cocoa makes it into the world markets each year. Adverse weather conditions such as drought will lead to slower growth, while too much rain can cause outbreaks of black pod disease. Brazil, another major producer, grappled in the past with a fungus called witch's broom that nearly decimated the country's cocoa crop in the 1990s.

Ripe, brown-speckled pods can be found on the tree throughout the year, but the main harvest starts in September and can last until early in the following year, causing prices to dip to their lowest between October and January.

Traditionally, cocoa is sold in the form of beans, which major buyers then process into chocolate, cocoa butter, cocoa powder, liqueur, etc. In recent years, in an effort to increase the value of exports, some producer countries, such as the Ivory Coast, Ghana, Nigeria and Brazil, have developed their own facilities for grinding beans.

The United States is the single largest importer of cocoa, followed by the Netherlands and Germany. Of the 2.8 million tons of cocoa produced every year, Europe consumes almost half while the US buys 0.4 million tonnes. The biggest names among the buyers are chocolate makers Nestlé, Hershey's and Cadbury, and food companies like Kraft.

The International Cocoa Organization (ICCO), which represents the producers of cocoa, is a good source of statistics about the crop. Cocoa futures are traded on the NYSE Liffe exchange in London and on NYMEX in New York.

Wheat

Wheat is the one of the most widely grown grains and the staple food of many countries.

As the number of people living on this planet rises so does the consumption of this grain, not only because more people need more bread but also because countries like China and India are becoming wealthier and are eating more meat than before. Cattle, pigs and poultry are raised on a mixture of corn, soybean and wheat and it can take 16 pounds of grains to produce one pound of meat.

The rising popularity of clean fuels such as biodiesel and bioethanol has become another new source of demand for grains. Corn is one of the most popular raw materials for biofuels; corn and wheat compete for the same farmland and when more acreage is allocated to corn, wheat prices move higher because less wheat is farmed.

Prices tend to dip during harvest times and as this grain grows well in most climates, price declines happen several times in the year. Countries with intensive farming like the United States and Canada produce two crops per year; the US winter wheat is ready for harvest from May to July and spring wheat from August through September. Russia and Ukraine, also known as the bread basket of Europe, harvest in July and August and supply most of the North African countries including Egypt, the largest buyer, and the Middle East. It is no coincidence that the recent revolutions of the Arab Spring coincided with high wheat prices.

The European Union is another big producer and acts both as an importer and exporter depending on the needs of the different countries.

Weather conditions are hugely important to the size of the crop, particularly at harvest times. The US National Centers for Environmental Prediction provide weather forecast maps for up to three months in advance, an invaluable tool when trying to assess how successful a harvest will be.

Wheat futures are traded in London, Paris and on the Chicago Board of Trade, their prices frequently moving in tandem with other grains like corn or soybeans as big funds tend to invest in the whole agricultural complex rather than only one type of grain. Apart from weather news, one of the biggest short-term price movers is monthly reports by the US Department of Agriculture which track how much wheat is planted both in the United States and around the world.

Soybeans

Soybeans were first cultivated in China about 5,000 years ago. The humble bean arrived in the United States in the early 1800s as a heavy material used to stabilise a clipper ship and first flourished in North Carolina because of its hot and humid summers. These days the US, Argentina and Brazil have taken over from China as the major producers of the crop and Brazil is expanding soybean farming with such speed that the USDA estimates the country will become the world's largest producer by 2016.

In the United States the soybean is now the second largest crop behind corn, having recently overtaken wheat. Soybean farming is concentrated in the country's grain-growing belt stretching across Illinois, Iowa, Minnesota, Indiana, Nebraska and Ohio.

Soybeans mature relatively quickly, taking between 100 and 150 days from planting to harvest. In the US, soybeans are planted in May and June and harvested in the autumn. Over 90 per cent of all the soybeans currently farmed in the United States and two-thirds of what is farmed around the globe is genetically engineered. The popularity of GE soybeans comes from its resistance to disease, which has reduced the cost of herbicide spraying by 50–80 per cent, resulting in much lower farming costs.

The soybean is used not only for human food such as in tofu and imitation dairy products but also as animal feed given to poultry and pigs and more recently to some types of farmed fish. Outside the food industry, soybeans are also used in the production of soap, cosmetics, resins, plastics, crayons, solvents and biodiesel. The three big growers, the United States, Brazil and Argentina use soybeans as the raw material for biodiesel production, while countries like Indonesia, Malaysia, along with the EU, use palm oil and rapeseed oil. China is the biggest consumer of soybeans. It imports almost 60 per cent of the globally traded beans, with the 27 countries of Europe coming a distant second.

Soybean futures and options are traded on the CME, the Dalian Commodity Exchange in China and the Tokyo Grain Exchange. It is also available as a futures contract in Brazil and Argentina, India and South Africa. Although the volume of futures traded is highest in Dalian, the contracts there are much smaller than in Chicago, with Dalian trading contracts of less than 400 bushels and CME contracts of 5,000 bushels of No. 2 yellow soybeans. Soybeans are graded by number (usually one to four) and are defined as either mixed or yellow. The underlying soybeans traded into the futures markets are yellow, and usually grades one to three are represented. Grade two yellow soybeans prices are considered the benchmark for soybean futures contracts. The Chicago contract is traded in dollars per pound and will usually form the underlying price for spread betting.

The summer months are typically the most active and volatile. Excessive heat or floods in America's Midwest will have a significant effect on prices. Another big market mover is the monthly crop reports published by the US Department of Agriculture around the 10th of each month.

The US Department of Agriculture publishes two other sets of reports that are key for those who trade soybeans. The first is the Prospective Plantings report released around the end of March, at the beginning of the soybean growing season, and which summarises how much of the crop farmers expect to plant in the coming season. The second is the Grain Stocks report which provides information on the current supply of soybeans and other grains both in the United States and the rest of the world.

Why I like commodities markets

Many experienced commodities traders would never look at any other financial market. This is because commodities share some characteristics that are unique to this asset class, and bring with them price dynamics that some traders and spread bettors like.

1 Commodities are *real* assets: you may be spread betting using a price informed by the underlying futures markets, but at the end of that financial chain is a real commodity, be it a barrel of oil, an ingot of silver or a bushel of wheat. It is something that is produced, and is bought, sold and often consumed.

2 The confidence factor that is so important to a government bond or a share price is not part of the commodities game – it is instead all about supply and demand. How much is being produced? How much is being consumed? Is it being delivered on time? What is interrupting production and delivery? How much is it costing to get it out and refined?

3 Commodities are political – certainly – government debt is political too. But these days, commodities prices bring down governments, force high-level resignations or cause governments to slam down export restrictions. If global politics is something that interests you already, that can help to inform your take on commodities prices.

4 Commodities are important – without commodities, our daily lives would grind to a halt. Commodities play a key role in everything we do on a daily basis, be it making a cup of coffee, turning on a light or driving to work. We are all consuming commodities all the time, and the demand for them is only becoming fiercer as the rest of the world industrialises at break-neck speed. This, more than anything else, will make commodities a critical financial market over the next few years, and with that will come the price action traders seek.

6

Forex – the world's biggest financial market

Foreign exchange or 'forex' markets have been opened up to the private trader in a big way thanks to financial spread betting. Forex is one of the most liquid financial markets in the world: literally trillions in currency changes hands every day between banks, fund managers and other participants in the fast-moving world of currency trading.

The first thing to bear in mind when spread betting forex markets is that there is no central exchange to buy and sell forex on. The market is made by institutions buying and selling foreign exchange, most of them for fairly practical reasons. There are, of course, plenty of speculators in the market too! But the lack of a central exchange means the foreign exchange market never sleeps: you can trade it all day and all night if you want. It is arguably the favoured market for night owls and insomniacs. Just because the UK stock market is closed for business doesn't mean you can't get a price on the British pound.

The second point about forex is that you never trade one currency in isolation. You are always trading a currency pair. You will usually see currencies quoted using three-figure abbreviations – for example, the UK pound is usually referred to as GBP by currency traders. A currency pair will show you two abbreviations. For example:

GBP/USD   1.5990/1.5996

This is the number of US dollars it takes to buy one British pound. As you can see, spread betting companies will usually quote currencies several figures past the decimal point. This is because the relative price of currencies will shift only incrementally (usually) over days or weeks, so the real price action has to be far to the right, several decimal places away.

As with all spread bets, you won't be quoted a single price – you still have the same bid and offer price as with all other financial markets. Here's another one:

USD/JPY   81.14/81.20

Because there are many more Japanese yen to the US dollar, you don't need to be trading so far to the right of the decimal point for your price action, so here the spread betting company is only giving you two digits to the right.

Currency trading is big business, which is quickly winning favour with the spread betting community, and this is why:

■ Round the clock trading, with no worrying about when the market is going to close.

- Highly liquid markets, which means it is relatively easy to get the price you want – the forex market is just so large, it is easy for spread betting companies to hedge their exposure and find the price you want.

- Highly efficient markets – you don't need to worry about sudden company news taking your position out. Currencies will move on the news, and move quickly, but by comparison with share markets, they are relatively transparent.

- Relative trading – somewhere there is always a currency on the rise, even at the worst of times; they can't all fall together.

So what are you trading when you are buying or selling a currency? Remember, with spread betting you are really only trading the price you are quoted by the spread betting company, you are not buying real currency in the real market. But your bet will be affected by how that currency moves.

A currency is really a benchmark of the relative health of a country's economy. Bear in mind that many currencies have not been free to trade for very long: global foreign exchange markets as they exist today only started in the 1970s as various governments began to abolish fixed exchange rate mechanisms and floated their currencies. Central banks, which are responsible for the management of a country's currency, still occasionally try to manipulate their currency by buying or selling large quantities of it, or simply by printing more of it. Recently we have seen a number of countries seeking to keep their currencies cheap in order to keep their countries economically competitive. The US Federal Reserve, the United States' central bank, has been injecting more dollars into circulation in order to keep the US currency cheap. The Japanese government has similarly intervened in global foreign exchange markets to keep the yen above 80 to the US dollar.

The currency majors

It is worth mentioning the US dollar at this juncture, as this is still the world's *de facto* reserve currency. This means that more central banks around the world hold dollars than any other currency (other than their own, of course). Things are changing, with banks selling dollars in favour of some other currencies, but if they were ever forced to go public with which currencies they hold, you would find most of them sitting on a veritable pile of dollars. This also means that traders tend to focus on currency pairs in which the dollar is one side of the trade. A typical spread betting company will see the vast majority of its forex trades involving the dollar.

In the world of currency trading, there are really only three currency 'majors', namely the dollar, the euro and the yen. If China were ever to allow its currency to float freely, it might join the majors, but we're unlikely to see that happen any time soon.

Most forex traders will therefore be trading USD/JPY or EUR/USD. These are the heavily favoured currency pairs. On top of this, there is also plenty of traffic in GBP/USD and AUD/USD (an interesting currency pair, as the Australian dollar is roughly on a par with the US dollar). Beyond this, there are several other currencies which are sometimes traded, such as the Swiss franc, the Canadian dollar and the Scandinavian currencies. Some spread betting companies now offer a fairly eclectic range of currencies, including Polish złoty, Turkish lira and Israeli shekels, but you will need to look closely at the spreads for these, as they may not be as liquid as some of the currency majors.

What moves currency markets?

Like other financial markets, currency markets are constantly on the move, but they are driven by different news and information flows than share markets. Sometimes they will react in the same way, but not always. Here are some of the more common types of announcement to look out for when following a currency:

Central bank and fiscal policy statements

Governors of central banks and finance ministers sometimes make public speeches and other announcements which can include observations that will move currency markets. Some forex analysts can get obsessive about the movements of central bank governors, their habits, body language, even the colour of tie they are wearing, seeking some kind of indicator as to what they are likely to do next in the monetary policy stakes. In Britain, the speeches made by the Chancellor of the Exchequer to Parliament are closely watched, as these can contain important policy announcements which will affect UK borrowing and the strength of the pound.

Inflation figures

Inflation can seriously harm an economy. As US president Ronald Reagan once said, 'Inflation is as violent as a mugger, as frightening as an armed robber, and as deadly as a hit man.' We have been lucky enough to live in an environment where inflation in the world's large economies has been largely kept under control, but that may not last forever. At time of writing, for example, economists were becoming increasingly concerned that the Chinese economy was over-heating, recognising the importance China has as a major importer and exporter, the *de facto* workshop of the world.

Inflation can harm economic growth, as it means people will be earning less in real terms, and can afford less. Runaway inflation, as occurred in Germany in the 1920s or more recently in Zimbabwe, can be particularly harmful, but even rates in the 10–13 per cent range can cause an economy to suffer. It is hard to believe now that the UK inflation rate in 1975 was 24.2 per cent. Yet from the end of the recession in 1992, until the beginning of the credit crisis, UK inflation rarely crept above 3 per cent. However, forex traders and economists continue to worry about inflation – ultimately, if you hold a currency issued by a country with 10 per cent inflation, that currency will be losing 10 per cent of its value for every year you hold it.

Interest rates

Central banks are usually vested with the power to set base rates, certainly among the currency majors. In the United States, this is the responsibility of the US Federal Reserve (the 'Fed'), in Japan it is the Bank of Japan, in the Eurozone it is the European Central Bank (ECB), and in Britain it is the Bank of England's Monetary Policy Committee. Interest rate announcements are scheduled, and the information released publicly across all the newswires at the same time. Analysts are now becoming very skilled at predicting interest rate moves, and it has been some time since any of the major economies has caught them by surprise. The credit crisis and the global recession have led to an environment where rates have been kept close to zero while central banks have pumped additional money into the global financial system. The Japanese interest rate has remained close to zero ever since that country's economic bubble was popped in the early 1990s. Other countries, however, have higher rates. Australia, for instance, was the first major economy to start raising its rates in the wake of the global recession.

You will sometimes hear forex analysts talking about the 'carry trade': this is a strategy where investors will borrow money in a currency with a low rate of interest – the yen for example – and deposit it in a currency with a much higher rate of interest. In the past decade, a favourite was to borrow yen and buy New Zealand dollars. This led to a trend where the NZD/JPY currency pair became a favourite for forex traders, as the NZD strengthened specifically against the JPY.

Unemployment figures

The number of people out of work is an important indicator of how well an economy is doing. If the jobless number is seen to be falling, it can be a buy signal for traders. Many governments report their jobless figures on a monthly basis and the markets will wait for these numbers and react accordingly. Jobless figures can be difficult to predict. In the United States, it is the Bureau of Labor Statistics which is responsible for announcing the jobless rate. Because the US is still the world's largest economy, many forex traders will watch these numbers closely. Remember, many traders also have a position either long or short the dollar, so anything which is likely to affect the US economy will be of interest.

Trade figures

Governments regularly release numbers on how much international trade has passed through their ports. This gives traders a good idea of whether that country is buying more than it is selling, or selling more than it is buying. Trade is important to a currency, because anyone trading with that country is going to need to buy or sell its currency in order to do business. A trade surplus (you are exporting more than you are importing) is seen by economists and traders as a good thing, a sign of a strong economy. Some economies are more dependent on their global trade flows than others, and their currencies can sometimes reflect this. New Zealand, with its large agricultural exports, and Australia with its mining industry, are both countries with currencies that can sometimes reflect the strength – or weakness – of their export markets.

Manufacturing figures

Some governments also publish manufacturing figures, which are viewed both as good indicators of the demand for manufactured goods domestically, and of the demand for a country's exports. In Britain, for example, the Bureau of National Statistics publishes manufacturing data on a monthly basis. Some major economies also have manufacturing benchmarks which are published on a regular basis, to give investors an idea of what the leaders of manufacturing businesses are thinking. In the United States, it is the closely watched monthly survey conducted by the Institute of Supply Management (ISM). In Japan, the Bank of Japan's Tankan survey, which is really just an indicator of the number of big Japanese manufacturers reporting positive conditions, is an important signal for the yen. Bear in mind that there are always forecasts of the likely results of these surveys ahead of time – the reaction in the currency markets will be sharper if these forecasts are wildly off the mark.

Central bank intervention

Central banks have different mandates from their governments, but they share many of the same objectives. Focusing on keeping inflation down and managing interest rates are two responsibilities shared by many central bank governors. In the current environment, central banks are competing to keep their currencies cheap in order to help their economies dig themselves out of a recession. The Bank of Japan (BoJ), the Japanese central bank, intervened in the currency markets in 2010 by selling yen. The yen had been appreciating against the euro and the US dollar as investors bought it as an alternative to the troubled euro or the US dollar. The Japanese economy relies heavily on its exports, and when the yen rose to a 15-year high against the dollar, the BoJ acted by selling some of its own yen holdings in sufficient volume to bring down the price again. This demonstrated to traders its commitment to protect the currency, and made them think twice about going long yen – they could not be certain that the bank would not act again. Central bank intervention of this kind can cause very sudden turns in the value of the currency, because unlike interest rate announcements, they are not scheduled and can catch the market by surprise.

Credit rating

A country's credit rating will affect its ability to borrow money on the global capital markets, a point I will return to in Chapter 7 on spread betting on bond markets. Two major ratings agencies, namely Moody's and Standard & Poor's, issue ratings on a country's bonds. Many market participants take these ratings very seriously, as an independent measure of the strength of a country's economy, and any downgrade will likely lead to the currency also being sold off.

Other news

Obviously, other news can very quickly have an impact on currencies. For a currency major, it would need to be something fairly substantial. For example, the Japanese tsunami in March 2011 was expected to cause a sell-off in the yen. Instead, it had the opposite effect. In the immediate aftermath of the disaster, many currency analysts were predicting the yen would fall against the dollar, but they did not check for a historical precedent. In 1995, following the Kobe earthquake, the yen strengthened as many Japanese companies and insurance firms repatriated assets, buying yen and selling foreign currencies. In 2011, forex traders ignored analysts and began buying yen in expectation of a yen rally.

It is extremely difficult to react to an official announcement after the fact. Even though it is now possible to execute a spread bet in the space of seconds, big FX investors will, inevitably, always be faster, and you will be highly unlikely to benefit from any resulting move in a currency. The increasing use of high frequency trading strategies means the professionals will always be able to trade more quickly than a retail trader. Prices will move before you get a chance to react. Hence, it is best to take your position in advance of the announcement, based on what you think it will be.

Take UK interest rates for example: some traders I have spoken to who have been able to consistently predict whether the Bank of England (BoE) will raise or cut sterling rates, reach this point by studying the minutes of the Monetary Policy Committee, which are published on the Wednesday of the second week after the interest rate meeting they record. They also follow a handful of highly rated FX analysts, such as Philip Shaw at Investec (whose comments regularly appear in national newspapers). This gives them a good grasp of which way the Bank of England is likely to move. Consequently, they are rarely surprised.

Currencies in brief

The US dollar (USD)

The US dollar or 'greenback' remains the *de facto* reserve currency of the world, despite the trials and tribulations of the US economy in 2007–09. It has enjoyed this status since the 1940s, and while there are proposals being aired in some quarters about an alternative global reserve currency, the US dollar continues to rank top among currency traders. Eighty-five per cent of currency transactions around the world involve trades with the US dollar.

The USA remains the world's largest economy, it is the number one importer and number three exporter, and despite the fact that China has now overtaken Japan as the second largest economy, the margin between second and first place is huge. Economic figures released by US government agencies are closely watched by currency traders. Apart from the interest rates set by the US Federal Reserve, the USA's central bank, other key economic statistics affecting the US dollar include Non-Farm Payrolls (NFP), the US trade balance and various measures of consumer confidence, such as the US Consumer Confidence Index, calculated by the Conference Board.

The euro (EUR)

After the US dollar, the euro (EUR) is the most widely traded foreign currency, and the EUR/USD currency pair is arguably the forex trade that sees the most activity on any given day. The euro is the latest and the most ambitious attempt at a currency union so far, and is used by 13 countries inside the European Union, with Estonia being the latest addition on 1 January 2011. It is also used outside the EU, for example as the currency of Montenegro.

The so-called Eurozone represents one of the largest and most prosperous economic blocs in the world. Interest rates for the euro are set by the European Central Bank in Frankfurt, and are closely watched by traders. But because the Eurozone is so economically diverse, it remains hard for currency traders to decide what the right price should be for the euro: economic figures released by the German government are still considered valuable, but they do not speak for the Eurozone as a whole.

The euro was introduced onto global foreign exchange markets in 1999, three years before it became available in coins and notes. Although it suffered initially due to a lack of confidence on the part of traders and a severe downturn in the French and German economies in 2001–03, the euro has rallied in the decade since, and was recently close to parity with sterling.

There continues to remain a great deal of speculation in the financial media about whether the euro will be able to survive the current European sovereign debt crisis, or the Eurozone break up into smaller currency blocs. While some European governments continue to struggle financially, it has been a popular currency to short against other, stronger currencies such as the Canadian dollar or the Swiss franc. However, the EUR/USD pair remains one of the most popular currency pairs to trade and a good potential starting point for new currency traders.

The Japanese yen (JPY)

The Japanese yen is one of the most popular trades in the global currency markets, and considered one of the currency 'majors'. It is the most widely traded Asian currency, even though the Chinese economy is now technically larger than Japan's. Because it is not possible to trade China's currency, the yen continues to feature high on the list of most currency traders' shopping lists.

The yen was floated as a freely tradable currency in the foreign exchange markets in 1973. In the 1970s it depreciated to around JPY300 to the US dollar. With the growth of the Japanese economy in the 1980s, the yen soared, becoming the darling of many currency traders. In 1985 it had reached 80 to the USD. Although the Japanese economy spectacularly crashed in 1989, the yen has continued to feature in many currency trades, and recent weakness of the euro and the dollar has seen the yen return to levels not seen since the mid-1990s.

The yen's share of global foreign exchange reserves has been on a steady decline since the early 1990s as banks diversify into other currencies. It reached a low of 2.9 per cent of global foreign exchange reserves in 2007, although it has since increased its share at the expense of the euro and the US dollar.

The British pound (GBP)

The British pound, also widely known as sterling, is the fourth most traded currency in FX markets, after the Big Three (the US dollar, the euro and the Japanese yen). The pound is also favoured by central banks, which frequently keep a substantial allocation of sterling on their books.

Ever since the euro was introduced, UK governments have continued to be vexed with arguments over whether the country should join the euro bloc, but so far Britain has resisted.

The decision in 1997 by Tony Blair's Labour government to allow the Bank of England independent powers to set UK interest rates means that the pound has become less susceptible to the sorts of politically inspired crises that have affected the currency in the past, like the 1976 sterling crisis (when Britain was bailed out by the International Monetary Fund (IMF)), or the forced withdrawal of the pound from the European Exchange Rate Mechanism (ERM) in 1992.

The pound is most frequently traded with the US dollar (the GBP/USD currency pair is often referred to as 'cable' by FX experts on account of the transatlantic cable that was once used to communicate currency prices in the days before satellites) as well as with the euro. The European Union remains the UK's biggest trading partner, followed by the United States.

The pound is regarded as a relatively responsibly managed currency at the moment, and FX investors have a high degree of confidence in the track record of the Bank of England in managing the currency since 1997. The Bank has been tasked with keeping UK inflation rates below 2 per cent and the governor of the Bank of England must write an open letter to the Chancellor of the Exchequer (the UK finance minister) every month it fails to do so.

More recently, however, the Bank has embarked on a process of 'quantitative easing' designed to help stimulate the UK economy by printing money to buy up debt. This has led to higher interest rates, but with UK base rates already so low, it has few other options.

The Swiss franc (SFR)

The Swiss franc (SFR) has long been considered a currency for institutional investors to buy when they need to get out of riskier assets, particularly during times of financial crisis. Heavy buying of the Swiss franc will happen at times of stress, when investor confidence in other assets like shares or commodities is ebbing.

Switzerland has traditionally been regarded as a conservative, neutral country where it is safe to keep your money, hence the success of its private banking industry. Switzerland has also steered clear of EU membership and the Eurozone. It is this neutrality policy of the country's successive governments that has led to its currency being favoured by investors.

The Swiss franc was backed by gold reserves to the tune of 40 per cent, a legal requirement laid down by the Swiss government, but this was abandoned in 2000 following a referendum. In recent years, it has traded very closely to the euro, maintaining a rate of approximately 1.55 to the euro. Switzerland remains heavily influenced by the economic fortunes of the Eurozone, as it is surrounded by Eurozone countries and counts the EU as its primary trading partner.

The Swiss franc will tend to rally at times of political turbulence, not just when there are financial problems. Look for it to gain strength against other major currencies when there is increasing political instability on a global scale. It is not particularly popular among central banks, and has rarely accounted for more than 0.3 per cent of global foreign exchange reserves in the last 20 years. The Swiss franc is more popular with private investors than central banks, who still make use of bank accounts denominated in the currency, even though the macroeconomic case for holding Swiss francs is less powerful than it was in the late 1990s.

The Australian dollar (AUD)

The Australian dollar is one of the two major 'resource' currencies, the other being the Canadian dollar. Australia is a major producer of raw materials, particularly base metals, and as such its currency has been boosted by increasing global demand for its products. After the Japanese yen, the

Australian dollar (also referred to as the 'Aussie' by currency traders), is arguably the most widely held currency in the Asia Pacific region, and is ranked number five in the world in terms of daily volume. In 2010, it accounted for 7 per cent of total global FX trading volumes.

The Aussie has been around since 1967, when Australia left the sterling area following the British pound's devaluation against the US dollar. It only became a free-trading currency in 1983, when Australian prime minister Bob Hawke cancelled its previous peg to a basket of other currencies.

Forex traders like the AUD for a number of reasons, including Australia's exposure to the commodities price cycle, to the booming Asian economies (Australia has been a direct beneficiary of China's economic growth) and the fact that it is not one of the Big Four currencies most commonly traded. The currency tends to perform worse during bust cycles, as global demand for commodities slumps, but outperforms the more popular currencies in boom times. Australia was the first major developed nation to start raising its interest rates in the wake of the 2007–08 crisis. Australia also never entered a technical recession during this period.

Australia has an independent central bank, the Reserve Bank of Australia, which is responsible for setting interest rates. Currency analysts and economists favour Australia because of its sound monetary policy and its political stability, as well as the AUD's correlation with resources prices.

The Canadian dollar (CAD)

The Canadian dollar (CAD), also known by veteran traders as 'the Loonie' because of the aquatic bird on the one dollar coin, is one of the two main resource-driven currencies. Like the Australian dollar (AUD), it is heavily influenced by the prices of the major commodities which Canada exports. As commodity prices go up, so often does demand for the CAD. Canada's main trading partner is the United States, so it is the USD/CAD currency pair that gets most attention from traders.

Canada's economy is heavily dependent on the raw materials the country produces, including timber, grains, base metals, gold and oil. It is also a major producer of potash, an important agricultural fertiliser. Seasoned CAD traders will follow commodities prices closely to try to gauge trends in the currency.

The Canadian dollar was first floated in 1950, although its rapid fall against the US dollar (USD) in the years 1960–62 led to it being fixed for a period.

It floated again in 1970, and parity with the USD was achieved in 1976. The CAD was cheap against the USD for much of the mid- to late 1990s, but has come back against the greenback over the past decade, achieving parity with the USD again in 2007, and the USD fell as the United States went into recession. The CAD is held as a reserve currency by a number of central banks, particularly in the Western hemisphere, where it is favoured by central banks in Latin America and the Caribbean.

Canada follows a transparent free-market system. Its interest rates are set by the Bank of Canada, the central bank, which is tasked with keeping inflation low and promoting the economic well-being of the country. The bank's governor is appointed by its directors, with the approval of the Canadian cabinet.

Emerging markets currencies

Some spread betting platforms now provide access to emerging markets currencies. There are a wide variety of emerging markets currencies available, including Czech koruna (CZK), Polish złoty (PLN), Turkish lira (TRY), Israeli shekel (ILS), Singapore (SGD) and Hong Kong (HKD) dollars, and even the Brazilian real (BRL). A currency will generally be made available to FX traders if there is enough demand and enough liquidity in the underlying interbank market. It also has to be free to trade. Some currencies, notably China's yuan, are still not freely available and unlikely to be anytime soon. China protects its currency jealously, and the yuan's relative cheapness versus the US dollar has become something of a political hot potato between Beijing and Washington, DC in recent years.

Emerging markets' currencies tend to come in and out of favour with spread bettors, and the vast majority of FX trades placed with a spread betting firm on any given day will tend to be among the three majors, with a relatively high volume trading sterling as well (although these days the GBP is not ranked as one of the premier currencies). For example, the Polish economy was one of the few European economies to perform well in the immediate aftermath of the credit crisis, and this led to some speculative activity on the long side of the Polish złoty.

Traders also like these 'fringe' European currencies because they hope that one day they will join the Eurozone – being judged suitable for Eurozone membership is a major stamp of approval for FX traders and other investors. Although the Polish government has said it hopes to join the Eurozone in 2012, the problems surrounding Greece and the future of the euro bloc mean choppy times ahead for the złoty and other European currencies with Eurozone ambitions.

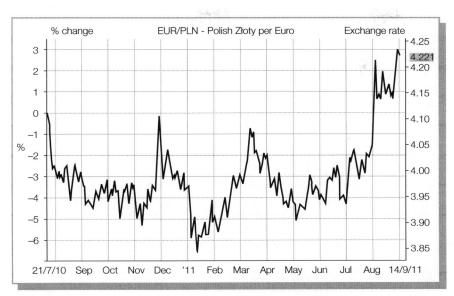

www.alphaterminal.co.uk
© Alpha Terminal

Figure 6.1   **EUR/PLN 2010–2011**

www.alphaterminal.co.uk
© Alpha Terminal

Figure 6.2   **EUR/USD 2007–2011**

As you can see from comparing the two charts Figures 6.1 and 6.2, the sheer volume of trades being transacted in EUR/USD provides for a much smoother trend if you were looking to bet against the euro than EUR/PLN. The złoty is significantly more volatile and prone to sudden moves. But, on the other side of the coin, you can benefit from some big price moves, as in the second half of 2008, when investors were exiting the złoty at high speed. Because there were fewer participants in the market, the big sell-off in emerging markets' assets as the credit crunch took hold had a major impact on the złoty, producing a big price swing for those long the euro against the Polish currency.

When trading emerging markets' currencies, be aware that you may have to pay for a higher rate of margin, and see wider spreads than you might be used to with the EUR or USD. This is because there is simply less of that currency being traded globally – there are far fewer złoty in circulation than US dollars. Emerging market currencies can also be more volatile than the majors, with sudden changes in price, so be sure you protect yourself with stop losses.

What is XAU/XAG?

You will sometimes see XAU or XAG quoted as part of a currency pair on some spread betting platforms. XAU is gold quoted as a currency, and XAG is silver. These currency pairs, for example XAU/USD, let you trade a currency against gold or silver. We looked at these precious metals in more depth in Chapter 5 on trading commodities markets, but hundreds of years ago they were used as a currency themselves, and within living memory, currencies were still linked to the gold price. The US only left the gold standard (which allowed for US dollars to be converted into the equivalent value in gold held by the Federal Reserve) in 1971, and as recently as 2000, 40 per cent of Swiss francs in circulation were backed by gold.

So why trade a currency pair like XAU/USD (see Figure 6.3)? There has been increased interest in trading gold against currencies in the last 18 months as the gold price has strengthened. Precious metals, because of their historical status as stores of value and currencies in themselves, have gained in value against paper currencies as central banks have printed more money to facilitate quantitative easing. Quantitative easing is the process by which a central bank buys financial assets like bonds in order to inject more money into the financial system. It does not actually print new physical bank notes, but it does create the money it uses to acquire the assets. Traders and central banks know there is only a finite supply of precious metals out there in the world –

the mining industry can only dig up and refine a small amount of gold every year. Central banks can't print gold. In addition, gold is not subject to the same inflationary pressures as paper money. This has led to a situation where some FX traders have wanted to trade gold against the US dollar in particular. They wanted to exploit what they saw as a strong trend of declining dollars and rising gold prices.

What to trade

When getting started in forex trading, it is best to trade one of the major currency pairs, and some FX traders never go beyond this. They find they get all the price action they need in these highly liquid markets.

The most popular currency markets for spread betting are EUR/USD and GBP/USD. After that USD/JPY is frequently traded, along with the so-called

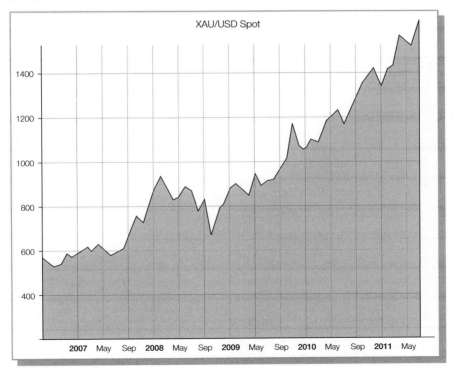

© ProRealTime.com

Figure 6.3   **XAU/USD 2007–11**

resource currencies, AUD, CAD and NZD. Most traders like to keep the USD on one side of the trade, because it is the global reserve currency and a benchmark for many FX traders and analysts.

Once you become more experienced, you may want to branch out into other markets. For example, you might seek out particular developing trends based on technical analysis, and this may lead you to markets where there is no USD component – GBP/JPY for instance. Or you may want to strip out your USD exposure completely. Some currency markets can end up range-bound for quite some time, leaving the experienced FX trader with little scope to make money. A range-bound market is one that moves between two price points, an upper and a lower one. The market lacks any real momentum, and the price tends not to break out of the trading range.

Ultimately, much will depend on your style of trading, your own personal psychology, and your risk tolerance.

7

Spread betting on debt and interest rates

One of the markets most neglected by spread bettors is the bond markets. Bonds are not everyone's cup of tea, and as with other spread betting markets, it is important to understand that with a spread betting account you are only trading the price of bonds, not actually holding bonds yourself.

Most spread betting companies quote prices on the major global bond markets. As with currencies, these have historically been very liquid and very efficient markets, making them ideal for spread betting. However, the range of markets remains fairly limited, largely because this is what spread betting consumers want: they like to trade the main benchmark government bond markets, and are not interested in anything else.

Some spread betting companies now offer the facility to spread bet the price of corporate bond indexes, which represent the performance of the debt of a collection of leading companies. Some firms also claim to be able to quote prices on bonds issued by individual corporations, although this may be a case of phoning up and asking, as they're unlikely to be listed on the main trading platform.

Beyond government bond markets, it is also possible to spread bet on the money markets, speculating on changes in the rate charged by banks to lend to each other in certain currencies, mainly the US dollar, the euro, sterling and the Swiss franc.

What makes bond markets tick

Bond markets are massive. Governments finance most of their national debt by issuing bonds. Each bond issue has a maturity date – the date when the bond issuer has to pay everyone back, and an interest rate (or coupon) – the rate of interest that government or company is obliged to pay out. Any larger government running a debt will be issuing bonds on a regular basis to finance that debt, particularly as older bonds reach their maturity dates.

Bond markets, like currency markets, are driven by a number of factors, and if you are planning to spread bet bond markets, it is important that you know what these are. The most critical are:

National debt

How much is the government borrowing already, and how big is its total debt compared with the annual output of the country's economy? Traders and investors like to have some kind of idea of whether a government can afford its debt.

Spending

How is a government spending its money? Is it doing so wisely and acting with financial prudence, and how likely is it to manage its finances properly?

Taxation

How much is a government taking off its people in terms of revenues, and will this be enough for it to continue to meet its debt obligations?

Risk ratings

Government bonds issued by the leading economies have typically been rated as AAA by independent ratings agency Standard & Poor's (which rates all government debt issues around the world). Other ratings issued by Moody's and Fitch are also important, and any pronouncements made by these agencies are taken very seriously by the market, and have the capacity to move bond markets significantly.

Political changes

Elections and personnel changes at the highest levels of power can affect bond prices; markets can take a view on the overall competence of a government or a finance minister. Right of centre governments tend to be seen as better bets for bond investors, but not always.

Appetite

When governments auction their bonds, they are depending on the appetite of investors to help price the bonds and determine their coupon. Some governments are lucky to have fairly placid domestic investor communities composed of tame pension funds and banks which will habitually buy up most of a bond auction. Japan, for example, has been able to manage its massive debt on the strength of domestic buying, while smaller economies like Ireland rely heavily on foreign investors. The less appetite there is for an auction, the more expensive it will be for a government to borrow. The bid-to-cover ratio – the amount by which an auction is over-subscribed by investors – is a good general indicator of appetite. A ratio of less than 1 will indicate that the government has failed to auction off all its debt, although governments are generally careful to avoid this eventuality (excess is often simply bought by the government itself, for example via a national debt purchase programme).

Bond markets are all about the credibility of a country and its government – like any other credit market, where one party is lending to another, the ability of the borrower to pay back his loan is critical. The US government, for example, has been able to ramp up its debt over the last decade or so on the strength of the size of its economy, its AAA credit rating, and the overall transparency and credibility of its government, not to mention the willingness of overseas buyers like China to continue to buy US treasuries.

How bond markets are priced

Remember, when spread betting, you are trading on the change in the price of bonds. You are not receiving the interest paid out to holders of actual government debt. This is because spread bets are inspired by the price of underlying futures contracts, which in turn are based on bond prices. As a spread betting customer you are already two steps away from the bond market.

You will most typically see a spread bet based on bonds priced like any other futures contract, with some kind of expiry date – for example, '10 yr treasury March 2012'. As with other futures contracts, this means your spread bet will expire at the end of March 2012, or you can pay a small fee to roll it over into the next contract.

Bonds are usually tracked according to their yield, although on a spread betting platform you will usually see their price. The yield is the proportion of the face value of the bond that is accounted for by the interest rate. If yields are going up, it means the price of bonds is going down and vice versa.

Hence, a US 10 year treasury note issued at $100 and 5 per cent coupon might drop by $2.50. Now the yield on the bond has changed. That $5 the bond would pay out is worth more than 5 per cent of $97.50 (it is actually 5.13 per cent). The yield has gone up while the price has gone down.

Investors view AAA-rated bonds as a source of income. As someone spread betting these markets, you are trying to gauge investor demand for the bonds in question – as with all other financial markets, the more demand, the higher the price. If the yield falls below the coupon, then investors are paying more for the bond than they would have done at auction. As someone spread betting this market, you just need to worry about the price of the current contract.

Traditionally, investors would buy bonds as a safe haven for their money, and many pension funds, banks and governments still keep a large proportion of their portfolios in bonds. However, times are changing. The credibility of some G10 countries, and of their outstanding debt, is being called into question in some quarters. The US Treasury worries that one day China may lose its appetite for US debt.

On top of all this, we have a flight to quality by investors in Europe, fleeing Greek, Portuguese and Irish debt markets. Uncertainty has injected a new level of volatility into bond markets, as sovereign debt is no longer seen as the sure bet it once was. This could make these markets more interesting from a spread betting perspective, albeit more volatile as well.

The main bond markets

US treasuries

The US 10 Treasury bond is the most widely quoted debt instrument used to measure the performance of the bonds issued by the US government. Called 'treasuries', US government bonds are issued by the US Treasury and are considered the most secure government (sovereign) debt it is possible to hold. Many governments and pension funds hold large quantities of these bonds.

Ten year treasury prices are a good measure of how the market views the health of the US economy. Their performance is affected by a wide range of economic factors, among them the interest rates set by the US Federal Reserve, levels of unemployment, the level of overall US government borrowing and the strength of the US dollar. Any benchmark of US economic performance, including speeches made by key policy makers like the Chairman of the Federal Reserve and the US Secretary of the Treasury, will affect the price of the 10 year bond.

Despite the high levels of borrowing by the US government, and the lack of real growth over the past few years, the US economy is still the largest in the world by a significant margin, and there is a high degree of confidence on the part of international investors that the United States will not default on its foreign debt obligations. China, Japan and Britain remain the largest holders of US government bonds.

Some spread betting companies will sometimes quote prices for treasuries of other maturities, for example the five year bill.

UK gilts

The UK 10 year bond is the benchmark British sovereign bond and its price is the one followed most closely by those who trade UK debt markets. UK government bonds are often referred to as 'gilts', reflecting the historical levels of confidence in the UK economy. Traditionally, bonds issued by the Bank of England had a gold edge, and the term has come to refer more generically to bonds issued by governments with solid credit ratings.

While the UK Treasury, which is responsible for managing Britain's debt, issues bonds with a variety of 'maturities', it is the 10 year bond which is most closely followed, and which you will see quoted most often as a spread betting contract. There are other bonds issued by the UK of various maturities, but fewer firms will quote prices on these. Online trading companies tend not to quote daily cash bets on sovereign bonds like the UK 10 year. In addition, their daily points move will tend to be fairly small, requiring substantial leverage to make any appreciable profits from a trade.

Traders of the 10 year gilt price will focus on a range of factors, including indicators of the health of the UK economy and its levels of borrowing. Among these are speeches made by the Chancellor of the Exchequer and the governor of the Bank of England, levels of unemployment, inflation statistics, interest rates and estimated levels of economic growth.

The UK is still a member of the G10 group of large economies, and its debt is still rated as AAA by Moody's, the international ratings agency responsible for assessing sovereign and corporate debt.

Japanese government bonds (JGBs)

Japanese government bonds or JGBs are the most popular market for government debt traders in Asia. The 10 year bond issued by Japan's Ministry of Finance tends to be the price tracked by most spread betting companies, although JGBs are issued with a range of maturities, from two out to 40 years. The 10 year bond is also used as a benchmark to measure the level of demand for other Japanese sovereign debt, like 20 or 30 year bonds.

Prices of the 10 year JGB will fluctuate according to political and economic feedback coming out of Japan. In particular, this will include statements made by the Japanese government about its level of borrowing and taxation. The level of take up or appetite for new bond auctions carried out by the Ministry of Finance will also have an impact on prices.

Japan is one of those lucky countries with a relatively tame local institutional investor base. This means that many new bond auctions are snapped up by large Japanese banks and pension funds, and the Japanese government has less of a problem financing its debts. However, Japan is one of the most heavily indebted of the G10 countries, and without this cushion it would have to pay much higher rates of interest for its debt.

Ultimately, all government or sovereign bonds are measured according to the market's perception of the ability of that government to settle its debts when the time comes – i.e. when debt tranches mature. Japan, despite its debt burden, is still considered one of the more stable issuers. Investors in Japan will also switch out of shares into bonds when they feel the economic or political picture in the country is starting to look more unstable. They will view JGBs as a defensive asset in times of turbulence.

Despite the inability of Japan's business sector to recover from the spectacular collapse of the economy in 1989–90, Japan's conservative political scene and large economy make its sovereign debt an attractive asset to own when other markets are taking a hammering. It is a market that investors will frequently turn to when other Asian positions look less attractive.

German bonds (the Bobl, the Bund and the Schatz)

Within the Eurozone, it is the debt issued by Germany that is most widely sought after by investors. German government bonds go by different names, depending on their maturity dates. The German government debt market therefore breaks down into three components:

- *Euro-Schatz*: very short-term debt, with a maturity of between 1.75 and 2.25 years
- *Euro-Bobl*: medium-term debt, usually with a maturity of between 4.5 and 5.5 years
- *Euro-Bund*: longer-term bonds, with a 10 year maturity. This bond is considered the benchmark bond for debt issued by the Eurozone, as well as for the German government bond market in general.

Germany's is the largest economy in the Eurozone, and as such its bonds are in most demand from investors. The spread between the yields of German bunds and their equivalent issued by other Eurozone governments is often quoted as a measure of market confidence.

Money markets

It is also possible to spread bet interest rates futures. These are bets based on futures contracts, which in turn reflect the market's anticipation of where base interest rates might be three months out. It is a way to speculate on whether you think base rates in a particular economy are likely to rise or fall in the next three months.

Short Sterling

The most popular of these markets is Short Sterling, which is based on futures contracts trading in anticipation of Bank of England base rates. The price of the bet is inverse to the base rate – i.e. it is 100 minus where the market thinks the rate would be.

For example, if the market thinks the BoE base rate will be at 1 per cent in three months – a not unreasonable speculation at time of writing – then the Short Sterling rate will be around 99. Because not everyone will agree on this, the price will fluctuate up and down a fair bit. Spread betting firms will quote a price two decimal points to the right, so you won't be betting on just the figure 99, but 99.06 or 98.97.

Up until recently, spread bets on Short Sterling have not seen high volume, as it has been obvious that the BoE has been keeping interest rates steady at 0.5 per cent while it has been ushering through its process of quantitative easing. As it begins to seek to bring UK inflation under control, and speculation over a base rate rise increases, expect to see more activity (and volatility) in Short Sterling.

In summary, the Short Sterling contract provides you the trader with the opportunity to bet on which way interest rates are likely to go.

Euribor

After Short Sterling, Euribor is another popular money market spread bet. This is based on the European Interbank Offered Rate, the unsecured lending rate between banks in the euro area. It is determined by a panel of European banks, which publish their daily lending rate. The most extreme 15 per cent quotes at either end of the range are eliminated, and the remainder are averaged to provide the overall figure. This is usually quoted out to three decimal places.

Euribor is an extremely important money market rate, which is affected by a range of economic circumstances, including the European Central Bank's base rate, but unlike Short Sterling, this is not a rate based on a central bank rate. It really reflects overall liquidity and confidence within the European banking system. In the second half of 2008, it dropped from over 5 per cent to less than 1 per cent in a matter of months, a spectacular move for those traders who were able to short it, and keep their margin facilities in place at the same time!

Eurodollar

Back in the bad old days of the Cold War, after the Soviet invasion of Hungary, the Russians needed to keep their holdings of foreign currency – most of it in US dollars – in bank accounts outside the United States (they were afraid the US government would seize their money). They unwittingly jump-started the Eurodollar market, the practice of keeping US dollars in banks outside the United States.

Eurodollar futures – and the underlying spread bets – reflect the market's anticipated rate for interbank lending of US dollars three months in advance. Like Short Sterling, it is a bet on where the rate is likely to be. It also reflects the cost of borrowing US dollars from banks outside the United States. The Eurodollar market is considered to be the most widely used loan market in the world. This makes it efficient in terms of pricing, and highly liquid, and therefore a market favoured by major traders like funds and banks.

The Eurodollar rate is based on LIBOR (London Interbank Offered Rate), a widely used interest rate benchmark for commercial loans. In the case of Eurodollar spread bets, these are usually based on the three-month rate (the rate also used by the Chicago Mercantile Exchange for its Eurodollar futures contract).

The LIBOR in turn is calculated every day by a panel of banks in London, and is based on the rate of their cost of funds in the dollar market that day. It changes throughout the day, but the quoted rate is the average rate fixed at 11.45 in the morning. When spread betting, however, your price is being informed by the price of the futures contract, which is where the market expects Eurodollar LIBOR to be when that contract expires. You are not betting on today's Eurodollar LIBOR. Hence you will see the price fluctuate second by second, not change once a day.

Euroswiss

The Swiss franc has often been considered a refuge currency during times of extreme economic turbulence. This was partly because of the perceived prudence of both the Swiss government and its banks, and Switzerland's political neutrality. It remains to be seen, post-credit crisis (when even some Swiss banks ran into problems) whether Swiss franc deposits retain their allure.

Like other money market rates, the Euroswiss contract is usually based on where the market expects lending rates for the Swiss Franc (CHF) to be in three months or on contract expiry. Don't get confused however between the Euroswiss money market rate and the 'Swissy' – the EUR/CHF currency pair, which can also sometimes confusingly be referred to as 'euroswiss'.

Summary

The key points to bear in mind when spread betting money market rates:

1 You are betting on a price inspired by the underlying futures price, although probably not the exact futures price – it is where the market expects the rate to be when the contract expires, not what it is today;

2 The rate is based on what a panel of banks expects to be able to borrow on, in that currency, from other banks;

3 The rate is usually expressed as 100 minus the actual rate, so a 2.5 per cent rate might be expressed as 97.5;

4 The price is often quoted out to three decimal places: for example 99.375: your tick rate will be the figure on the end.

8

Technical analysis

Once you start researching financial spread betting you will quickly come across people using what will seem like a bewildering array of charts and graphs to analyse markets. This process is known as 'technical analysis', and the people who rely on charts for their investment decisions are sometimes called 'chartists'.

Technical analysis has been around for some time now, but it is gathering more adherents every month. The more traders there are who use technical analysis to buy and sell, the more accurate it becomes, as everyone uses the same factors. It is almost a self-fulfilling method of following markets.

On its own, technical analysis is not going to turn you into a millionaire overnight. It is really a tool to help you to determine when to enter and exit markets, and when a trend you are following is likely to reverse. In this chapter we will look at some of the more widely used charts. It is the tip of the iceberg really. There are hundreds of different theories out there about how to analyse markets. If it is something you would like to learn more about, further ideas for reading are provided in Chapter 11.

'Technical analysis is the study of past trading data with the aim of forecasting the future direction', according to Michael van Dulken, a research analyst at Accendo Markets. This is possible via the identification of the signals given out by the price, volume and an array of secondary indicators, which together, display the underlying psychology of market participants and trend of the price.

The background to technical analysis

Technical analysis in Western financial markets was really born with the observations of the US stock market made by Charles Dow in the early 1900s. Dow was part-owner and editor of the *Wall Street Journal*. He observed that the US share market tended often to move before news that affected it became available. Looking at the market in aggregate, it was unthinkable that the entire market could be manipulated in this fashion. Ergo, it was potentially possible to predict price movements in advance of news, or indeed in advance of the major moves. This in turn began to reinforce the case for studying price movements in a more technical fashion, on the strength that, beyond individual stocks, and over longer periods of time, the price should reflect all the market news.

There is not the space here to explore efficient markets theory – other publications have already done a good job of that – but the crux of what Dow and his successors were after was a means to catch trends and reversals early, before the rest of the market piled in. Too often we hear stories about how retail traders are always the last to buy into a bull market, just as it peaks, leaving them, more often than not, saddled with a loss. We hear about the canny hedge fund managers who are first into a market, and make millions thanks to their prescience; but much of this boils down to being an astute observer of the markets, and using the right tools to assess them.

At its most basic, technical analysis involves looking at resistance and support indicators. A typical market will often move between two price levels – an upper (resistance) and lower (support) limit. It will seem as if whenever it reaches the support level, it will take off again, and will top out as it gets to the upper limit. Why is this? you may wonder. Is there a big seller out there automatically off-loading stock whenever the price hits a certain level?

The reality is, many market participants, including professional and amateur traders, funds, banks, market makers, you name it, are all looking at the same prices: resistance levels (a particular price point at which the market is likely to turn from an upward trend back to a downward one) and support levels (the exact opposite – the price below which the market could reverse direction as more buyers come in). Resistance and support levels also act as 'floors' in a market – they are a means of forecasting when there is a likely change of direction, even though this may not change an overall trend. If a trader is focusing on short, intra-day price movements, they can still be important indicators.

These levels apply as much to share markets as they do to commodity or forex markets. The reason they exist is because they represent the price beyond which the market will buy or sell as it perceives the price becoming too high or too low. It is not just one big trader causing this (although there are some examples in the history of financial markets when it has been), it is hundreds or thousands of traders all reacting the same way.

In the end, a market can become 'range-bound' – effectively bouncing between two price levels. If it breaks beyond one of these – a 'breakout' – it can cause excitement, as traders and analysts come to the conclusion that the price is moving on towards a new resistance level.

Resistance levels are important when spread betting; one is tempted to scoff at them initially, but they are very real, and need to be watched closely. Without other fundamental news to drive prices, resistance levels can begin to dominate things, as traders focus on particular price levels. They can often be nice round numbers, because that is how humans think. Gold at $1000, the FTSE at 6,000 points, the Dow at 10,000 points, these are all famous resistance levels, but most markets and shares will have their own resistance levels.

In the case of shares, resistance levels may also exist because a market maker, a firm charged with buying and selling a company's shares and maintaining its liquidity in the market, may be using resistance levels as its own buy or sell signals. It can have a powerful influence over the short-term course of the price of smaller or mid-cap shares. Of course, a bad set of company results will thwart any market maker trying to support a resistance level!

Japanese candlestick charts

Japanese candlestick charts have been used in East Asia since the 1600s, when they were first employed by rice traders. They have only been used in the West relatively recently, first being brought to the attention of analysts by Steve Nison in his 2001 book *Japanese Candlestick Charting Techniques.* These charts are not for everyone, but I've found that once you start looking at markets with candlesticks, you never go back.

A Japanese candlestick is a measure of what the market did over a certain period of time, be it a minute, an hour or a day. It really depends on which

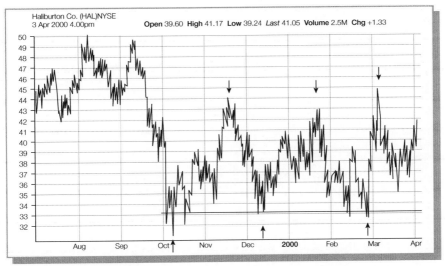

© StockCharts.com

Figure 8.1   Haliburton share price showing resistance levels and breakouts

timescale you are viewing the market from. A single candlestick will show you four pieces of information: the highest point the price reached during that time period, the lowest point, and the open and closing prices.

The top and bottom of the fat part of the candlestick are the price the market opened, and the price it closed. The narrow line goes as high as the highest price point reached, and vice versa, the line beneath traces the lowest price. Thus, if your market closing price was also the lowest price, you would not have a 'tail' to your candlestick. A very long candle is indicative of plenty of volatile moves, while a short, fat one is an indicator of a market that did not do much.

I say opening and closing price, as if talking about a single day in the market, and certainly you could look at a share market in this way, with each candlestick representing a single day. However, many analysts use them for shorter timescales, with the candlestick representing an hour or a 10 minute interval. When analysing forex markets in particular, where there is no market close *per se*, a candlestick is a useful measure of what has been happening on an hour-by-hour basis. As you can see, candlesticks provide you with much more information than simply a line on a chart.

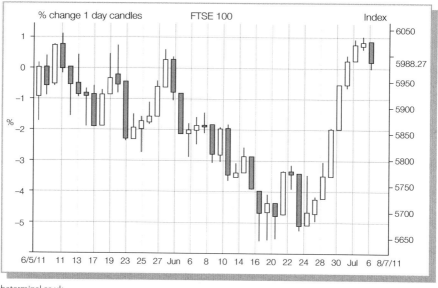

www.alphaterminal.co.uk
© Alpha Terminal

Figure 8.2   **Sample Japanese candlestick graph – FTSE 100**

Moving averages

A moving average (MA) is a line calculated using the average of past prices, but updated every day (or hour, or minute, or second, depending on the time period you are using). Taking a 20 day moving average as an example, your program is creating a line where each price point is the average of the prices of the previous 20 days. Other popular time periods are the 50 day moving average, and the 200 day moving average. The moving average helps the trader to identify a trend. If a price moves below a 20 day moving average having stayed above it for a long time, it might be a sell signal. In combination, two moving averages – the 20 day and the 50 day for example – can provide a higher conviction indicator that a trend has been broken, and a market is about to suffer a reversal. If, say, the price crosses the 20 day MA *and* the 50 day MA, then the market may well be heading for a fall.

The above are also referred to as simple moving averages, because there is also another type – the weighted moving average. This type of MA will place greater emphasis on more recent price activity. It seeks to skirt around the problem that simple MAs suffer from – they rely heavily on historical data, and are not as quick to react to reversals. Impatient traders and analysts who want to be able to react faster to possible changes use the weighted moving average to give them the extra time to exploit a move in price before the rest of the market.

Finally, an exponential moving average will take into consideration all the prices in the data series, but the earlier data is given far less significance than the most recent prices.

Traders will use a combination of MAs to determine whether they are really seeing an emerging new trend, or just a false dawn. If there is a crossover, with the price crossing multiple moving averages, this can be a buy or sell signal (depending on which way the market is moving).

MACD (moving average convergence/divergence)

The MACD is an oft-quoted measure of momentum. It takes a pair of moving averages, and subtracts the short-term one from the longer-term one in an effort to create a momentum indicator. The analyst is trying to identify some signal of underlying momentum in a market. It is meant to be able to identify both trend and momentum, hence its popularity. However, it is not considered to be a useful way to calculate whether a market is overbought or oversold.

Traders using the MACD will be looking for signals to get into or out of a market, including crossovers. For example, they might use the MACD with a moving average of the MACD (called the 'trigger' line). When the MACD falls below the trigger line, this can indicate it is time to sell. When it climbs above the trigger line, it could be time to buy.

The MACD tends to be favoured by analysts focusing on equity markets, rather than other types of financial market. Having said that, some commodities and forex traders claim to have enjoyed success using the MACD as well.

Bollinger bands

Bollinger bands are most often used as a way to analyse what a market is doing in the short term, for example intra-day. Most technical indicators are more efficient when used to identify trends and reversals over longer time periods. Bollinger bands are created using an exponential moving average (see moving averages above) with two other lines above and below it based on the standard deviation of the market you are looking at.

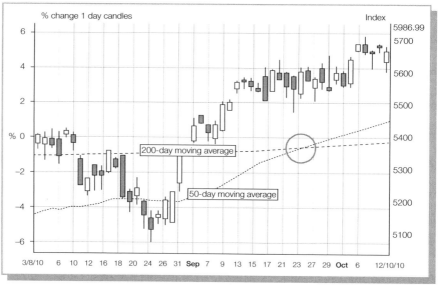

www.alphaterminal.co.uk
© Alpha Terminal

Figure 8.3   FTSE 100 showing 50 and 200 day moving averages and crossover

If the market becomes more volatile, the bands will get wider apart. If it starts to trade tightly, they will get closer together again. The key is where the price of the market is compared to the bands. If it starts to get close to, or even crosses the upper line, it may be time to start selling as the market is beginning to look overbought. If the price gets closer to the bottom line, it may be time to start buying.

Head-and-shoulders indicators

You will probably often hear chartists talking about the 'head and shoulders' of a market. This is one of the most popularly recognised patterns in financial markets, although there are many, many more, and not the space to go into them in this book. However, head and shoulders does seem to have caught the imaginations of many technical analysts out there.

A head-and-shoulders pattern looks in its purest form like just that: two smaller peaks, with a higher peak in between. Analysts will see one developing once a market has reached a peak and then dropped below the previous peak as well, and is then seen to be rising again. The assumption here is that the new peak will now be lower than the previous one. The market will not be able to achieve the same high again. Analysts will be

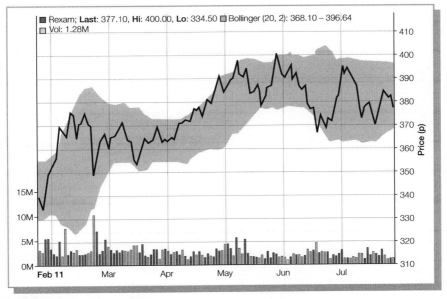

Figure 8.4   Bollinger bands

looking for the so-called neckline, a hypothetical line drawn between the dips on either side of the head. After the right shoulder has formed, they expect the price will go down.

RSI (relative strength index)

The relative strength index is a very popular measure used in conjunction with momentum – the speed at which a price is climbing or declining. Momentum is considered a better indicator of a bull market rather than a bear market, largely because markets tend to rise more than they fall – at least in the equities space. The RSI measures the speed at which prices are changing, again seeking that point where a market is overbought or oversold.

The RSI generates a figure of between zero and 100. If it is over 70, technical analysts begin to consider that market as overbought or 'toppy' and start to look for signs that it will turn. If it is below 30, it is starting to look oversold, and the price may be destined for an upturn. The RSI can sometimes be used in conjunction with other technical measures, like momentum or moving averages, to really look through the price action to find what is really going on with this particular share or market. It is used to try to filter out the 'noise' of a price jumping up and down, to discover what it is really doing.

Figure 8.5   Head-and-shoulders pattern

ADX (average directional index)

The average directional index was designed by Welles Wilder, an American engineer, to analyse commodities markets, but as with many technical indicators, it can be used across a wide range of financial markets. It measures the momentum of a market, but what it does not tell you is whether the market is going up or down – all it is saying is that the market is moving. The ADX is quoted in a range of 0–100. The higher it is, the more momentum you will be seeing. The lower, the more range-bound that market now is. Generally speaking, if it is over 20, there is a trend in the market. If it drops below, the market is losing direction. You might see it cross the 20 or 30 mark as the market begins to take off, drop below it when it runs out of steam, and then pick up again as the market is sold off.

The ADX is meant to help traders identify a trend in its early stages, before it becomes readily obvious on a normal chart. It is meant to tip them off to an opportunity to enter a market, or indeed to get out of one once it has lost its momentum.

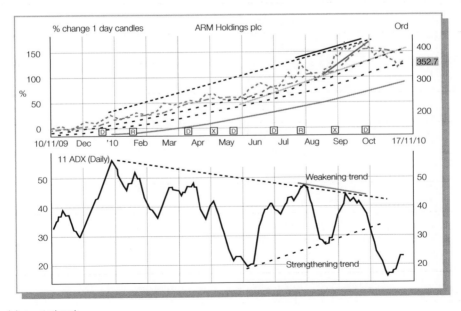

www.alphaterminal.co.uk
© Alpha Terminal

Figure 8.6   **ADX vs FTSE 100 showing possible buying and selling points**

Pivot points

Pivot points are often used in technical analysis to calculate support and resistance levels. A pivot point would typically be calculated using the averages of significant high points and low points of a previous trading period. There are a number of different methods used by charting programs to work out pivot points, and much will depend on which time periods you are using to create them.

Let's say you're spread betting the UK 100, you might then decide to use the daily behaviour of the UK 100 as your time frame. Each day would therefore have its own pivot point based on what the UK 100 did the day before. You could calculate it overnight or simply generate it at a touch of a button using a charting program the moment the market is closed at 4.30 p.m. Using the pivot points, technical analysts can also then begin to try and forecast resistance and support levels. Again, these levels will often be calculated using mathematical theories about markets, some of which are explained in more detail below. There is no completely accepted, carved in stone method of calculating pivot points, although there are a number that are in common use.

A common approach is to calculate a couple of resistance levels above the pivot point (e.g. one at 50 per cent and another at around 62 per cent above the pivot point), and a couple of support levels. This would then inform where you expected the market's turning points to be during that trading day.

Triangles

Triangles are often used when seeking a 'breakout' either to the upside or downside. They are drawn using a chart when the market looks like it is trading in an ever-narrower range, i.e. forming a triangle. It can be illustrated by drawing two lines, ideally with price peaks and troughs touching the long sides of the triangle two to five times. The shape of the triangle not only helps you to see what the likely breakout price would be, but it can also inform you about the trend the market is following. A bearish triangle will have a steeper upper angle, signalling that the market will likely break south before a certain point in time, while a bullish one will have the opposite.

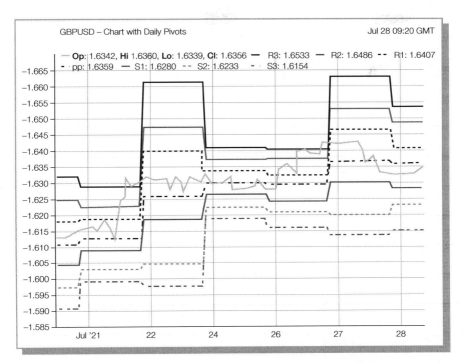

GBPUSD – Chart with Daily Pivots   Jul 28 09:20 GMT

Op: 1.6342, Hi 1.6360, Lo: 1.6339, Cl: 1.6356 — R3: 1.6533 — R2: 1.6486 -- R1: 1.6407
pp: 1.6359 — S1: 1.6280 -- S2: 1.6233 -- S3: 1.6154

© Action Forex, www.actionforex.com

Figure 8.7   **One week chart of FTSE 100 using pivot points, with sample resistance and support levels**

The theories behind technical analysis

Behind many of the more widely used forms of technical analysis lie mathematical theories that inform many of the ratios employed in charting programs. Luckily, in this day and age computers can do 99 per cent of the number crunching for you. But a great deal of the analysis discussed above is powered by mathematical assumptions pioneered by a number of twentieth-century market theorists.

Dow Theory

Named after Charles Dow, the creator of the Dow Jones Industrial Index, Dow Theory is one of the earliest forms of technical analysis. Dow Theory has come back into vogue recently, but over the last century plus it has swung in and out of fashion with technical analysts. On occasion, it has been used to accurately call the market to uncanny effect (for example by William P. Hamilton, editor

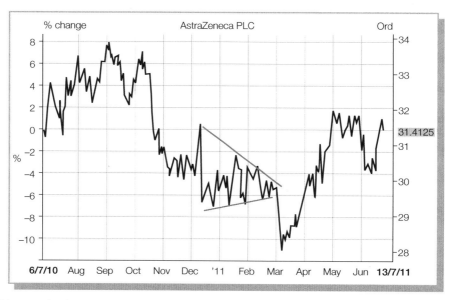

www.alphaterminal.co.uk
© Alpha Terminal

Figure 8.8   **Example of a triangle**

of the *Wall Street Journal*, a matter of days before the Wall Street Crash in 1929). It is not infallible, however. The core arguments of Dow Theory are as follows:

1   *Most of the information driving the market is in the price.* Something especially unusual and unanticipated would need to come out of the blue in order for the price to be affected otherwise.

2   *Markets are driven by three trends*: a primary trend which exists so long as the market continues to be able to reach higher peaks; a secondary trend of corrections, lasting between three weeks and three months; and a third trend of small corrections or ripples in the market. Obviously, it was to the primary trend that the likes of Dow and Hamilton paid the most attention.

3   Dow saw bull and bear markets occurring in three phases:

Bull market phases

■ **Early stage**: adventurous buyers come into the market seeking bargains; the best point in the bull market for canny traders to enter the market.

■ **Middle stage**: the bear market matures and more buyers pile into the market. This is when the price covers most of its upwards ground.

■ **Late phase**: the market is now starting to top out as latecomers buy in. Think of the NASDAQ at the very peak of the bull market in 2000, where retail investors were buying into internet and other technology stocks.

Bear market phases

■ **Early stage**: at the top of the market, volume in trading is still high, but the market has lost its momentum.

■ **Middle stage**: the newsflow turns negative and investors begin to sell. The price falls more often than it climbs.

■ **Later stage**: despite false corrections, the market is unable to meet previous highs. More investors are leaving. The newsflow has turned distinctly negative. Volume is now low, and the price is being driven by sellers.

4 *Lines*: bull markets in particular can conform to a horizontal trajectory for a while, but will then break out sharply upwards. They will tend to trade within narrow bands of around 5 per cent of the price while in this phase. It is less prevalent in bear markets, as optimism is draining out of the market.

5 *Averages*: Dow always used a secondary indicator to confirm trends. In his day, there were two established stock market indexes in the United States, the Industrials and the Railroads (partly because railway stocks composed such a large chunk of the US listed market circa 1900). He always looked at both indexes before he made a prediction, seeking confirmation of a trend from both before calling the market.

6 *Trends*: Dow looked for trends in the market, just as many traders and technical analysts do today. He was alive to possible reversals occurring as a market failed to beat previous highs and then produced some significant drops below the points established by previous reversals.

7 *Volume*: Dow was one of the first technical analysts to look at volume in the market. This could confirm whether the price was being driven by a lot of investors and traders, or only a handful. If the market is dropping, and the volume is high, with plenty of trading going on and shares changing hands, then you know this bearish move is a big one. If volume is light, and the price is moving, it may just be a false movement and not a significant trend.

Elliott Wave Theory

Ralph Nelson Elliott was an accountant who was forced to retire due to illness in the 1930s and began studying the stock market. He was a keen mathematician, and also familiar with Dow Theory. He argued that there were some fundamental mathematical principles behind everything in the universe, promoting natural patterns in physics, biology, astronomy and markets.

In the case of markets, he and his disciples have argued that bull markets move in five distinct waves – three upward trends (impulse trends) interrupted by two corrections (corrective waves). This in turn is followed by two downward trends, interrupted by a single bullish correction.

Elliott Waves need to be taken with a pinch of salt, as they don't stand up to rigorous scientific scrutiny. Some analysts argue that they only apply when there is solid underlying economic growth (i.e. the global economy is powering ahead, and not limping along as it was at time of writing).

Underlying Elliott Wave Theory are Fibonacci numbers. Fibonacci was a medieval Italian mathematician, who created a number series based on adding the two previous numbers together (1, 1, 2, 3, 5, 8, 13, etc.). It also creates a ratio by dividing one Fibonacci number by the one in front:

$2/3 = 0.67$

$3/5 = 0.6$

$5/8 = 0.625$

$8/13 = 0.615$

$13/21 = 0.619$

If you start dividing each number by the previous one, again after the first few numbers, you end up with:

$13/8 = 1.625$

$21/13 = 1.615$

$34/21 = 1.619$

And so on. The importance of this seemingly irrelevant exercise in mathematics is that Elliott Waves are meant to conform to Fibonacci ratios. Technical analysts will use these ratios to work out what price objectives will be in advance.

Returning to the original sequence of waves in the bull market, remember, Elliott claimed the bull market, regardless of the timescale being used, would break down into five distinct phases or waves, three up and two down, before the bull market ran out of steam. Let's assume you think a bull market is developing, and you want to use Elliott Wave Theory. You would take the top of the first 'peak' in your proposed bull, multiply it by the magic number 1.618, and add it to the bottom of the first 'trough' (i.e. the end of the first corrective wave). The theory goes that this should give you an indicator of where the peak of the next impulse trend will be.

To find the ultimate peak in the market, you would then take the height of the first wave, multiply it by 3.236 (1.618 × 2) and add it to the trough established by the first corrective wave.

In essence, the bull market is meant to conform to a 5:3:5:3:5 ratio sequence, while the bear will follow a 5:3:5 correction (although sometimes it will pursue what is known as a 'flat correction' of 3:3:5).

You will sometimes hear analysts talking about 'Fibonacci retracements'. This means they are applying lines to the chart based on these ratios and that they expect them to provide some kind of resistance level to the current move in the market. The usual ratios are: 61.8 per cent, 38.2 per cent, and a more prosaic 50 per cent. Each can be used to project a potential resistance level, whether the analyst is looking for a possible peak to a market (and therefore a price objective, a point where he may want to exit), or a point where a bear market is likely to correct and move upwards.

Gann Theory

William Delbert Gann was a cotton trader who made his name as a predictor of movements in commodities and share prices in the first three decades of the twentieth century. He has become somewhat of a legendary figure in chartist circles, partly because he was so successful, but also because he claimed many of his ideas were formed by his studies of ancient mathematics and geometry, including the designs of temples in India and Egypt.

Gann looked for mathematical, recurring patterns in nature and in astronomy, and based many of his ideas on the relationship between time and space. He famously predicted the price of a bag of wheat on 30 September 1909 would be $1.20, even though the market that day was still only around $1.09 an hour before the close. It rose to close at $1.20. The fact that Gann was being shadowed by a journalist at the time helped to reinforce his fame on Wall Street.

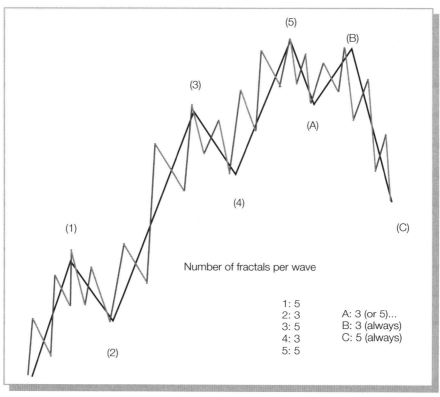

© AfraidtoTrade.com

Figure 8.9   Elliott 'cheat chart'

Gann (who died in 1955) was notoriously secretive about his methods, but over time, some of what he used has leaked out into the wider technical analysis community. For example, Gann angles are lines on a chart that are meant to help predict future turning points in the market. Gann argued that the price range from a significant low point to a high point is divisible by eight. A line can be drawn mid-way between these – the ⅛ line – which can provide a good indicator of possible support or resistance levels. The ⅝ level is considered the next strongest level.

Gann theories are often expressed as 'fan' lines – a series of diagonal lines on a chart that the technical analyst will use to provide him with a predictive edge. The ⅛ line can be drawn at exactly 45 degrees, while the next most significant fan lines can be drawn at 63.75 degrees and 26.25 degrees.

Gann used other theories to predict natural and political events. Here he crossed the line from what I would call scientific calculation into unfounded speculation. Some traders buy into this, others don't. Much will depend on how much weight you as an individual place on astrology. Suffice to say, Gann felt that financial markets were subject to the same universal laws of numbers as everything else. His results certainly indicate he was onto something.

Summary

Technical analysis is used by traders in the spread betting market to try to make sense of numbers, and of the market psychology driving those numbers. Analysts want to bring order to the sometimes chaotic jumble of lines and numbers that represent the various financial markets on a trading screen. They want to look for patterns they can act on. In this chapter I have really only scratched the surface of what can be a very intriguing and in-depth topic.

There is already a very considerable body of literature on technical analysis available for consultation, both online and in print (the bibliography in Chapter 11 contains some of the more significant works).

Much of the above analysis and calculation can, thankfully, be performed at a touch of a button; the charting facilities that exist on most sophisticated spread betting platforms will be able to produce most of the basic technical analysis you might want. This chapter should help you to begin to understand what some market analysts and chartists are talking about, but it is not essential to becoming a successful trader. Indeed, there are some traders who have been able to build perfectly good trading systems and go on to make a lot of money without any technical analysis whatsoever.

Technical analysis is a subject that those of a mathematical bent can find themselves becoming completely immersed in; it can be fun, but it can also be possible to over-analyse a market, and never actually place any trades – or make any money. Perhaps the best way to start down this road is to use a few indicators in the course of your early trading and see what works for you.

9

Finding your own trading style

Are profitable spread bettors born or made? It is a question that continues to engage trading circles. In 1983, a famous Chicago-based money manager called Richard Dennis bet his colleague, William Eckhardt, that it was possible to train novice traders from scratch. He recruited 23 people off the street, with no previous trading experience, and taught them how to become profitable traders. This was the beginning of his so-called 'Turtle' programme.

Not all of the Turtles succeeded, but enough did for Dennis to entrust them with millions of his own money, and for them to go on to generate over $175 million in profits in the next five years. A few went on to become successful money managers in their own right. You can read more about Dennis and this experiment in Curtis M. Faith's *Way of the Turtle*.

Dennis and Eckhardt both had a point. Dennis was not training his Turtles to find their own way to invest, he was teaching them to trade a system of his own devising. It was essential, he argued, to follow the system, to be disciplined, to avoid distractions, in order to profit.

More recently, BBC television broadcast *Million Dollar Traders*, which followed a similar experiment as a fly-on-the-wall documentary, with eight ordinary individuals being taught to become traders and in the end trade real money.

What both experiments illustrated was that while trading can be taught, not everyone is mentally suited to trade. Many people might think they are, but your emotional and psychological building blocks really determine your ability to trade – and to spread bet – successfully.

Having said that, there are many different approaches to trading financial markets, and it is possible that you may favour one approach over another. In this chapter we ask a few questions of you, the novice spread bettor, which may help you to find the spread betting approach that will suit you, your financial resources and your lifestyle.

How much can I afford to lose?

This is probably one of the most important questions you will need to ask yourself before you begin live spread betting. Before opening a spread betting account, it is crucial that you have a very clear idea of how much money you can afford to lose spread betting. What is the maximum loss you can sustain before you walk away? You will always need to have this in mind, because the last thing you want to do is to spread bet with money that you need for other things.

Money management is part of the discipline of being a good trader. Remember, if your initial pool of trading capital starts diminishing, perhaps after a few early losses, you will need to alter your position sizes to compensate. If you start spread betting with £5,000, and lose £1,000, then your position sizes will need to be 20 per cent smaller to compensate. Otherwise, you are ramping up your risk, and could suffer larger proportional losses later on. Your risk management must always inform your trading process, certainly in terms of the size of the bets you take on.

While working in the spread betting industry, it was repeatedly made clear to me that many people viewed spread betting as a way to make a quick buck. They would risk rainy day money, like a £10,000 college fund, for example, in the hope of making an additional few thousand pounds. They ended up losing cash which they needed for other things. Don't let this happen to you. Only spread bet with money you can afford to lose.

How much time can I devote to spread betting?

The amount of time you can afford to devote to spread betting will dictate your trading style. Many successful professional traders claim they spend 90 per cent of their time doing research, educating themselves about the markets, rather than simply sitting in front of a screen watching prices. You will see traders at big banks doing this, but that is because they are being paid to sit there by their employer. It is a popular misconception that the more time you spend sitting in front of a computer, the more likely you are to make money.

I once visited a trading company in Gibraltar which rented desk space and infrastructure to self-employed derivatives traders. It was interesting to see that some of their clients were spending all day in front of their screens, executing hundreds of individual trades, while others would come in first thing in the morning, catch up on overnight news, place a few trades (with stops in place, of course), and then go to the beach.

One of the reasons so many housewives are now successful traders is because they have the time and flexibility to match a trading program to their lifestyle commitments. They are often up early, so can put trades on before the school run, and can monitor their positions during the day.

This can also affect the sort of markets you like to trade. One of the reasons I like the currency markets is that they are open all night, and you can check up on them in the evening instead of watching television. You may prefer to trade US markets because they open at lunchtime in the UK, and close in the evening.

Your approach to spread betting will be dictated by the time you can usefully apply to it. Mobile technology now makes it easier to keep tabs on your positions while you are on the move, and can alert you to sudden changes, so there's no need to be anchored to your desk. But many people are able to sustain a successful spread betting strategy with only 30 minutes or so of focus time per day.

How do I behave under pressure?

'Know thyself', said the ancient Greek inscription at the Temple of Delphi, and this aphorism is particularly valid for spread betting. Don't kid yourself. Know your weaknesses. The markets will not – ever – cut you any slack. So it is crucial that you are honest with yourself when spread betting. In particular, how do you behave under pressure? Are you a risk taker, or would you describe yourself as cautious?

Some traders are over-confident. They can set off into spread betting in the belief that they are right, the markets are wrong and within months they'll be putting a down payment on a new Porsche. That rarely – if ever – happens. Some of the cleverest, most numerate people on the planet have been caught out by financial markets. If you feel you might be a tad over-pleased with yourself in your day-to-day life, be honest with yourself, and apply that to the way you spread bet. Ask yourself constantly whether this aspect of your personality is creeping into the way you bet.

Similarly, if you are a naturally cautious person, be aware of how this can affect your trading. Are you placing your stops too close to the market? Are you hesitating to put a trade on and then kicking yourself when it comes good and you weren't in the market? Are you getting out of your trades too early, and losing out on potential profits?

Those who may have a tendency to gamble anyway need to think very carefully about approaching spread betting. It may be considered in some quarters as gambling, but unlike gambling it brings with it additional risk factors in terms of the margin aspect. If you are the sort of person who nips in and out of betting shops on a regular basis, you may be best advised to stay away from spread betting.

How disciplined am I as an individual?

Trading requires discipline. If you are not a disciplined person, then you need to get strict with yourself when it comes to spread betting, because ultimately, it will be you who will carry the costs of poor market discipline. Once you have a trading plan in place, stick to it. Don't try to find ways around it, or argue yourself out of it. Once you begin doing this, it is a slippery slope towards disaster.

A very experienced trader once sat me down and tried to convince me that his losing position in the shares of an oil company was going to come good. He made a very complex case using technical analysis, but it was not convincing – most ways you looked at his position, it seemed as if it was going to lose more money. He was refusing to cut his losses, clinging to a share that would, in the end, cost him more money. He was looking to me to provide independent confirmation of his own technical thesis. He had already half-convinced himself he was right, but the reason he was doing this was the loss he had already sustained: he could not bear to 'wear' it, and instead was clinging to a losing position.

If you have a trading programme, and you stick to it, you are less likely to find yourself trying to convince yourself in the small hours of the morning that a losing position will come good. If you feel you are an undisciplined, lax or chaotic person, make sure you write a trading programme and stick to it religiously. There's nothing wrong with tweaking it later on, but again, be disciplined about when you tweak it. Don't change it just because that would suit where you are in the market right now. It is like being on a diet: no dairy products means *no dairy products*; not no dairy products, but maybe cheese on Sundays.

Let's say you decide to limit losses to a certain percentage of the total value of the bet, 5 per cent for example. You write in your plan that after exactly two months you will revisit it. After two months you notice that the market you are trading has rallied a fair few times just after you came out. You review your overall risk position, and decide you can tolerate a 7 per cent loss threshold. But you are doing this at the point when you decided to review the plan, not when you have a 5 per cent loss on a trade, and want to give yourself the opportunity to let it run.

Is spread betting going to be my career, my hobby or a way of making additional money on the side?

Have a clear idea of what it is you want to get out of spread betting. For me, it has always been an intellectual interest in financial markets, which is what got me into financial journalism in the first place. For others, it is a way to make some extra money, get out of the rat race or fill long bouts of insomnia.

Your trading strategy should be one that has a good chance of meeting your expectations. If you are going to only make a few hundred pounds extra per month, it is unlikely to be a way for you to ditch the day job. Be realistic about what it can achieve for you financially. With the best will in the world, you won't be able to turn a £5,000 spread betting account into £100,000 overnight. You will need to work hard at it, and it may take months or years. Spread betting is not like winning the lottery: it won't make you rich overnight.

Some people with large quantities of available cash are able to make big profits as well, but they start off with a six-figure account. Working up there from a smaller starting point will take time and a considerable dose of luck. On the upside, as a hobby, spread betting can be a lot more profitable than owning a yacht!

Am I a trader or an investor?

An investor is someone who buys something in the expectation that it will go up in value over time, may even pay them a stream of income, and can be sold for a profit at some yet to be determined point in the future. Investors like to accrue assets over time. They are astute money managers, often with a good eye for a bargain. They like shares, because they pay dividends and give them a share in a viable corporate entity. They like houses, because they are made of bricks and mortar and can be rented out to tenants.

Traders are focused on much shorter timescales. They think in minutes, days or weeks. They are looking for price action, the possibility for sudden, large changes in the value of assets. Traders like futures markets and spread betting because they don't need to shoulder the costs of owning an asset: there are no custody fees associated with a spread bet. Traders generally have a higher risk tolerance than investors.

Many investors venture into spread betting because it is often advertised or promoted alongside traditional investment services like share dealing. But some investors often find themselves unsuited to spread betting. Just because you have made a lot of money as an investor, does not mean you will be successful as a trader. There are some investors who also make good traders, but not everyone can be a Warren Buffett and a George Soros at the same time.

In addition, I would advise that if you are a successful investor, don't risk too much of your investment capital spread betting. With spread betting, you don't own anything. There is no underlying asset and no income stream. Your only profit comes from changes in price which, ultimately, the spread betting company controls. Such a scenario will make some investors go all wobbly at the knees! If your objectives are long-term capital gain, perhaps coupled with a degree of income, I would suggest looking elsewhere.

Approaching the markets

Day trading

In the 1990s the day trading phenomenon sprang up in the United States. Between 1992 and 2000, global equity markets were in a very long and very profitable bull trend. It was easy for many people with a solid chunk of starting capital to make money and earn a living by trading share markets. They were known as 'day traders' because they spent all day trading. Yes, it's that simple.

Today it is not quite as easy to make money in the markets. They are more volatile, and subject to pressures that did not exist in the 1990s. Prices are affected by market participants – like hedge funds, for example – that were much smaller and less influential 15 years ago. Day traders still exist, and many still trade for a living, but the day trading strategy referred to here is where a trader will close out their positions by the time the market closes. There are no positions held overnight.

As a lifestyle call, day trading can be attractive because it means you can spend some days trading, and some days on the golf course or doing something else more fascinating. You aren't worrying about what your spread betting account is doing while you're teeing off at the seventh. It also means that during those days where you are trading, you can be focused on the market.

From a psychological perspective, day trading is also useful if you're not feeling like trading when you wake up. You can leave the market alone and come back to it another day. It is also easy for day traders to determine how they're doing performance-wise: either they're up or they're down when they close out. The key is making sure there are more up days than down days.

Day trading strategies are necessarily very short term in nature. Some involve putting on a number of positions at the start of the day, while others deal with entering and exiting the market at the right moments in the course of the day (so-called intra-day moves). High frequency trading can be expensive when spread betting, however, as spreads can be so wide you will end up coughing up a big chunk of your gains. Be careful if developing a day trading strategy that involves dozens of trades per day unless the spread is amazingly narrow. You may find you end up with little real gain to show for it, although your spread betting company will be pleased.

Trend following

Trend following is one of the most popular spread betting strategies, and can work if you are a short-term or long-term trader, although most successful trend followers tend to lean towards the longer end of the time frame.

In a nutshell, trend followers use technical analysis to seek out trends in markets, and gradually build their exposure over time. If the trend looks like it has 'legs' to it, and will run, they increase the position. If it begins to look like it is running out of steam, they start to reduce their exposure. Trend followers tend to rely on moving averages as one of the key indicators of an emerging trend.

Patience is critical for the successful trend follower. They like to be fairly certain that a trend has emerged before they open a trade. This means giving up some early gains in return for the ability to ride the trend up (or down if it is a short trend). Once they become more pessimistic about the trend, they might close their original position and then open a smaller, more conservative position. This way they have managed to lock in some of the original value of the trade, and reduce their overall exposure in case the trend reverses.

Trend followers will shop around across a number of different markets in search of the right trend. However, there will be times in the markets when good trends are simply absent, and it will become very difficult to make money consistently this way. Some seasoned traders will take this opportunity simply to go on holiday, and come back when things have settled down. Trying to spread bet as a trend follower during periods of high volatility and market uncertainty is never a good idea.

Some of the great trends of recent history have included:

- The equity bull market of the 1990s: the FTSE 100 index set a new historical high in April 1991 and climbed steadily from there. The growth in the value of equities defined a generation of traders and money managers. The index only lost its momentum properly in December 1999, and by early 2000 it was becoming obvious that this particular mega-trend had run out of steam.

- The spectacular rise in the oil price from around $60 for a barrel of Brent crude to $144 in 2007–08. This was my most successful trade to date, as I reversed out of oil at $138 and then adopted a short position. Oil fell to almost $40.

- The rise in gold: the gold price climbed from $850 in the summer of 2009 to break $1,600 at the time of writing. In October 2009, a number of influential commodities analysts were arguing that it would not break the important psychological barrier of $1,000, or that if it did, central banks would unload some of their reserves to keep the price down. A trend seemed to be emerging north of about $925–950 as confidence in the euro and the dollar eroded. I went long gold once the $1,000 barrier was breached and the yellow metal moved significantly beyond that.

- The dramatic fall in the value of the pound in the final quarter of 2008 turned into a big earner for some foreign exchange spread bettors. Sterling fell against the euro, for example, from about 1.29 to almost parity at 1.02. The market for sterling then became much more choppy and unpredictable in 2009, and the trend evaporated almost before all the mince pies from Christmas had been eaten!

Swing trading

In the chapter on technical analysis we looked briefly at how some markets can become range-bound – i.e. the price never seems to break above a certain level, and seems to trade between two bands. This is the province of the swing trader, someone who uses the scope that spread betting offers to short markets as well as go long.

Swing trading in its most basic form involves going long the market until it approaches a resistance level, then getting out and eventually going short in the expectation that it will turn slightly before, or slightly after the resistance level. No market remains range-bound forever, so it is important that a stop loss is always in place to protect you when the price finally streaks out of the range.

Advanced swing traders use technical analysis and sometimes computer programs to help inform them about opportunities in the market. It is much more of a short-term strategy and many swing traders will be in and out of a trade in a matter of days. Unlike trend following, swing trading is more adaptable to volatile market periods.

Pairs trading

Pairs trading is a popular strategy with professional money managers like equity hedge funds. It is a strategy specifically used with shares rather than any other type of markets, although it has been used with some success with closely correlated indexes like the Dow Jones and S&P 500. In some respects, it is a kind of arbitrage strategy.

A pairs trader needs to find two stocks that trade fairly closely in tandem with each other. They might be in the same industry sector, for example, perhaps even close competitors. You would need to be able to identify a regular correlation in the price over a period of months or even years in an ideal case scenario.

I once worked with a team of software engineers building a trading program that would be able to predict the price of a share based on the prices of a basket of other shares that traded in close harmony with it. They needed to do this in order to be able to price derivatives contracts even when a share might be suspended on the stock market. It demonstrated that there are numerous occasions when two shares will be trading closely together. Sometimes shares will be seen to trade closely to certain commodities which the company relies on – gold miners and the gold price, for example.

The pairs trader is looking for the point where that correlation ends, where the shares diverge. When that happens, he goes short the share that is ticking upwards, and long the one ticking downwards. He is hoping that they will revert to their previous pattern of behaviour and consequently he will make money on both sides of the trade. Sometimes this is caused by temporary problems – for example a change of management, poor results, a takeover bid, director dealings, anything that might affect the share of one company and not the other.

Typical targets for pairs traders are big companies that are major players in their sector. Pairs trading can only really work if you can short a stock, which is why it can be used with a spread betting account but not a conventional retail share trading account.

Event driven trading

Event driven traders focus on market news. In its purest form, event driven trading involves trading the price of two companies involved in a potential takeover or merger situation. Conventional wisdom has it that the firm doing the taking over will see its share price fall as it often needs to borrow money to finance its acquisition, while the target company's shares will usually rise (not least because many speculators will be buying its stock on the news).

I've seen this strategy work well, and I've seen it go horribly wrong. But it still remains a favourite of some spread bettors, because it can drive share prices very quickly and create substantial profits for traders who know what they're doing.

In my view, event driven trading in the spread betting context goes beyond the mergers and acquisitions (M&A) space, particularly as there are periods, like 2009–10 for example, where there is little or no M&A activity in the market at all – companies are simply too busy staying afloat. But event driven traders also look at other events that can potentially drive prices:

- Trading government bonds and money markets can be extremely event driven: traders can take positions ahead of important economic announcements like interest rate decisions or economic data. There is usually a consensus view surrounding these, but it is not always right and markets can move quickly in the immediate wake of unexpected data. Interest rates have tended to be fairly predictable in recent years, but this could change as inflation picks up. The problems surrounding the US budget and the Eurozone's debt have also meant that political summits and meetings on Capitol Hill in Washington, DC have assumed more importance and are closely watched by markets.

- The energy sector and pharmaceutical sectors are particularly prone to events. I've seen plenty of activity in the share prices of individual mining and oil exploration companies in expectation of announcements of new discoveries. Humdrum share prices will suddenly rocket back and forth as news emerges about the success – or lack thereof – of a particular energy exploration firm. Traders in this area need to know the sector quite well and be following a number of different companies at the same time. It can be fairly labour intensive, but if you understand an industry – perhaps having worked in it – you can have an edge over many traders and stock market analysts.

▓ Because you are spread betting you can trade on bad news as well as good news. Few traders seem to be able to do this consistently – you almost require a 'glass is half empty' approach to life to be a good bear. A classic example was the explosion of the Deepwater Horizon oil rig in the Gulf of Mexico in 2010. The scale of the disaster for BP took some time to develop, but some astute spread bettors were able to go short on BP fairly early on – within 24 hours of the explosion. BP's share price fell from 601 to about 305 in a matter of weeks. It can be important to act early on serious bad news, because some spread betting companies will stop taking new bets once it becomes obvious a share price is plummeting. I saw this happen with Bradford & Bingley shares when the bank ran into trouble in 2009. Once the trend became very obvious, it was already too late, as many spread betting companies refused to take new short bets. It was becoming increasingly difficult for them to hedge the trade in the market.

It is worth mentioning here that by shorting a company on the back of bad news you are not harming the company. You are spread betting, not trading its shares in the real market. A spread bet is still just a contract between you and your spread betting company. If anything, the spread betting company will be trying to buy that company's shares in the market to hedge its risk. Spread betting activity can move underlying share prices a little, if enough clients are piling into a trade, and particularly if the company is a smaller one. But spread betting companies will often be taking the other side of the trade in order to balance their books.

Spread betting activity is not going to put a company out of business – companies are very good at doing that without any help from the financial markets.

10

Other types of spread bets

The spread betting industry never stands still. You will quickly learn that in a highly competitive market, companies will continue to innovate in order to keep your business. The most frequently used strategy is to compete on price or to provide special offers. But product innovation is another means of winning loyal customers. I fully expect to see more ways to bet on market moves appearing in the years ahead, as more people get involved in spread betting.

Although the vast bulk (80 per cent +) of spread betting volume takes place across fewer than 20 markets, the introduction of new markets and indexes is seen as one possible way of attracting new customers. For example, some firms already offer sector indexes, allowing you to bet on the average share performance in specific sectors, like the automotive or energy sectors.

Remember, some spread betting companies can be quite flexible when it comes to offering new markets, particularly with larger clients. But even if you are a small client, it is still worth asking for a market: if other punters are also requesting it, you may find dealers will quote a price. This is how many smaller companies end up on spread betting platforms.

CFDs

Most spread betting companies also offer Contracts for Difference (CFDs). They are very similar to spread bets, but they are priced slightly differently. You may wonder whether it makes sense to trade CFDs instead. Here are the key differences:

CFDs are not tax free

Unlike spread bets, CFD trading is not treated as gambling, and hence is not tax free. This means you will have to pay UK (or Irish) capital gains tax on any profits. It also means you may be able to off-set losses sustained in your CFD account against capital gains tax (CGT) in other areas. It is worth consulting an accountant, as the range of tax credits available in this area is large and complex. CFDs still have an edge over conventional shares, as there is no stamp duty levied on share transactions.

CFDs are priced differently

CFDs are not traded using the price per point system that spread bets use. Instead, a CFD will have a price at which you will buy it, and a price at which you will sell it (with the usual bid/offer spread, of course). Your profit is simply the difference in price. In many ways, it is more like buying and selling shares than spread betting.

Spread betting is not available outside the UK and the Republic of Ireland

You can't open a spread betting account if you are not resident in the UK or Republic of Ireland. In addition, if you move abroad, sooner or later you will be asked to close your spread betting account. CFDs are the next best thing to spread betting if you are living outside the British Isles. There are several companies – like Saxo Bank and Internaxx – which offer offshore CFD trading facilities. In addition, major spread betting companies like IG Index and CMC Markets also offer CFD accounts. If you are moving abroad, you may find you can simply switch to a CFD account with your existing provider.

CFDs were originally dreamed up in the investment banking industry, and are still popular with institutional investors like hedge funds and private banks. They are now widely used as retail trading instruments, and outside the United States they have become arguably the preferred retail financial derivative. At the time of writing, they seem also to have become the favoured tool for many private forex traders.

If you are not living in the United States, it should be possible to open a CFD account. The US is currently the only country I am aware of that has an out-right ban on retail CFD trading. Canada is in the process of authorising CFDs for sale within its borders on a province-by-province basis. In my experience, however, if you are living outside the US, even in countries without formal authorisation of retail CFD trading, you ought to be able to open an account.

In other respects, CFDs can be very similar to spread bets. The ability to trade CFDs on margin still exists, for example, and long CFD trades that are left open overnight will still be subject to a financing charge.

Binary bets

Binary bets are 'all or nothing bets' based like spread bets on movements in financial markets. A binary bet asks you to decide whether a market, like the FTSE 100/UK 100 for example, will close above or below a specific level. It may even be quoted with a certain time of day, not necessarily the actual market close.

The price of a binary bet will not resemble the price of the FTSE itself. Remember, you are only betting on whether it closes up or down, so the actual price has less relevance. The number quoted should be subtracted from 100, and the total multiplied by your stake.

Example

A binary bet on the FTSE might be quoted at 19/24 for 5750. If you staked £5 that the FTSE would be up at the bet's expiry (i.e. above 5750), you would be using the offer price of 24. If the market is over 5750 as the bet expires, you would win 100−24 = 76 (× £5) = £380.

If, on the other hand, the market was down, your loss would be calculated as 24 × 5 = £120.

As you can see, you lose much more than your original stake if you are wrong. However, your potential losses are more limited in a way, because you define your maximum loss at the outset when you determine your stake.

Binaries are available over differing time frames: you can bet on where the market will be in five minutes or in a week, for example. The range of markets is more limited for the more short-term bets, but the popularity of binary betting has meant that many spread betting companies have been adding to the available markets over the last couple of years. You can now bet on many of the major stock market indexes, the popular currency pairs and some of the key commodities markets. In addition, you can also bet on key economic indicators, like interest rates or US Non-Farm Payrolls, which is impractical for a standard spread bet.

Binary spreads will tend to be less than eight points, another factor that makes them attractive to spread bettors.

Apart from the conventional win/lose binary bet, brokerages now offer some new takes on the binary format, including:

Target bets

The bet pays out if the market closes up or down within a certain range. You might be betting on whether the bet will expire when the market is up 50–70 points, for example. If it expires north of the range, of course, the bet won't pay out.

Tunnel bets

Here you are betting the market will remain within a specific range during the life of the bet. A good example using the FTSE would be +/− 100 points. If the market trades outside this band at any time during the lifetime of the bet, you lose. If the bet expires without the market having traded outside the range, you win.

One touch bets

The bet pays out if the market ever goes through a nominated target level during the lifetime of the bet. It does not need to expire above the given level, just breach it.

High/Low (or 'Hi Lo') bets

These bets are usually based on what the market does today. You are betting on whether the high point or the low point is a given distance (or more) from the previous day's closing point. For instance, you might bet that the high point today will be 55 points higher than yesterday's closing price. You are less worried about what the closing price is, so long as at some point the high is beyond 55 points.

DIY bets

Also called custom bets, this is a potentially fast-growing and exciting development in the world of spread betting. It is more suited to the short-term market strategy, but it gives the trader more control over what the parameters are for the bet itself, particularly in the all-important risk quotient.

Custom betting seems to be geared more towards the short-term trader who is looking to make money off small, possibly intra-day movements in the market. It might be worth looking at if you are thinking more about multiple trades in and out of the market during a single day. Like binary bets, it is easier to nominate how much money you want to risk, and you are less likely to lose unforeseen quantities as the consequence of sudden market movements. It is a bit like binary betting, but here you have a bit more control over what you'd like to bet on (and the spread betting company will then quote you the price).

With the increased popularity of betting exchanges, which have expanded the scope of how and on what punters can now bet, it seems that this area of the spread betting market is destined to grow as well.

Is custom betting and binary betting real trading? In some respects, it feels more like a trip to the betting shop on the high street; you are simply betting on financial markets rather than horses or football. At the same time, however, financial markets can be slightly more predictable. There is an argument that a skilled trader could still make money using binary bets if he was used to intra-day trading and had a good feel for the market on which he was betting. He might see a trend emerging but still with a degree of uncertainty about it. He might therefore feel it was worth opening a binary trade which limited his risk, rather than a conventional spread bet.

Options

Spread betting options is slightly different to futures. As discussed in Chapter 1, spread bets started off using the futures contract format, because that was the underlying price that supported the price of the bet. Options in the real futures market give traders the right to buy or sell an asset or market at a particular price. But aside from futures, another popular form of derivative contract is the *option*. And options-style spread bets are now also being made available.

A *put* option lets you sell something at a given price, while a *call* lets you buy it. So, if you think the market is going to go up, and you want to be able to buy it at a cheaper level: a call option is what you want. If, on the other hand, you think the market will fall, then a put option lets you lock in a higher price than the one you expect will prevail in the future.

If gold, for example, was trading at $1,300, and you expected it to go to $1,500, you could buy a call option on gold at $1,350, for example. This would let you buy gold at $1,350 and sell it at $1,500 (if you were right, of course, and the gold market did climb).

If, on the other hand, gold was at $1,300 and you expected it to fall, you'd go shopping for a put option that would let you sell gold at $1,300 (or higher). That way you could buy gold at a cheaper price, and then sell it for a higher one.

An option, like a future, has a specific lifetime. At some point, if not exercised, the option will expire. In the options market, your counterparty is providing you with the right to buy (or sell) something up until a specific date. Once that date is reached, it is worthless, and expires. It is not like a future, especially a commodity future, where you might be expected to actually take delivery of an asset. An option just disappears like morning dew.

With a spread betting account, as ever, you are simply trading on the price of an option. You are not writing an option or being granted any particular rights to buy or sell something. You are just trading on a hypothetical. It is possible as a retail trader to trade real options, but that is a subject for another book, and there are plenty of good books on options trading available.

As with a binary bet, the price of the option will not be the same as the underlying market. It will indicate at what price the option can be exercised (the 'strike' price), but the price you should also focus on is the price of the option itself, or the 'premium' as it is known. This is what you are really betting on.

Example A

Spread betting a call option

Let's look at a daily FTSE call option.

Today's FTSE call option might be 15/18 (the bid/offer price) with a strike price at 5750. You note the market closed yesterday at 5725. You're feeling quite bullish (the FTSE has closed up every day for the past four days and you think this is a trend). You decide to buy the call option at £5 per point.

Let's take a look at your option premium first. Using the offer price, your premium – the cost of the option – is £5 × 18 (the offer price) = £90. This is the amount of money you would lose if the FTSE does not get to your strike price by the end of the day. And this is all you are going to lose. There is no scope for losing more with an option, which is possibly one of its big attractions for the risk averse. You are nominating your total loss in advance.

Let's say the market behaves as expected. When do you make money? Once the FTSE in this scenario crosses the 5750 barrier, you still have to account for your premium – in this case 18. After 5768 however, you would be 'in the money' for £5 per point.

Like other spread bets, you need to decide when to exercise your option. You don't want to hold it all the way to expiry. With this example, once your bet had crossed the 5768 line, you'd be making money, but you'd need to decide when to get out.

Example B

Shorting a call option with a spread bet

Because you are spread betting, you don't have to simply buy a call option. You could in fact sell it. In the above example, the price was quoted with a bid/offer of 15/18, which means you could open a short position. In this case, you are almost 'writing' an option (acting as the counterparty in the option trade).

When selling a call, you pocket the premium in advance. Taking the previous case, let's say you expected the FTSE would actually fall from its 5725 level. You could take the same call option quote, of 15/18, with the same strike price at 5750. Let's say in this case you use the same stake of £5 per point. You would be paid your premium of £5 × 15 (£75) when you opened the bet. You would be hoping the option bet would not be exercised before the end of the day.

However, there's a catch. What if you are wrong, and the market goes against you? You have no other profit to speak of from this trade, as you have already made it – £75 premium. If you're wrong, and the market ends up crossing the strike price threshold, you could potentially make a big loss.

Taking this example a step further, let's say the market rises 100 points – at 5785 you are already out of the money by 25 points (£5 × 25 = £125). Deduct your premium of £75, and you've still lost £50. The problem with shorting call options is that if you're wrong, the potential loss is limitless.

Usually, when a spread betting company offers options, it is quoting spread bets based on option prices. It is not offering you a separate options account. However, some bigger firms offer both, so it is worth checking.

Options are available on some of the big stock market indexes, the popular currency pairs and commodities markets, and also on some shares. Spreads can vary quite widely and won't tend to be as competitive as conventional spreads. On top of this, the long options, those out to a week or more, will tend to have wider spreads than daily options.

When spread betting options, you will tend to face shorter expiry dates than in the real options market, where you can buy options with expiry dates that are weeks or months away, but in return, real options trading will require much larger amounts of cash up front than spread betting.

11

Further resources

The range of resources available to the novice trader is enormous. In terms of the support available, and the amount of additional information available online, the new trader is better placed than ever before. Filtering out what you really need, and what will actually add value to your trading strategy, is the real task. Trial and error will help you find the resources that really lend themselves to what you are setting out to achieve with your spread betting accounts.

The spread betting companies

As a client of a spread betting company, you will have at your fingertips a really quite wonderful range of resources, some of which is now integral to the various spread betting platforms. This now includes:

- Live news and economic announcements via the newswires, something which costs professional traders thousands of pounds to have delivered to them on their desktops. News can be delayed by 15 minutes (much of the free news published by newswires on the internet has a 15 minute delay, as the real premium is having this information as it goes out, literally in less than a second). Having said that, the big newswires are now beginning to allow spread betting companies to broadcast their information on a live basis on their trading platforms.

- Additional technical analysis is now being liberally disseminated via email and YouTube by in-house teams of analysts. I find the information sent out by Accendo Markets to be particularly strong for its technical analysis of UK stocks and the FTSE indexes, while Saxo Bank currently offers excellent daily forex coverage and analysis. Many traders will have a favourite analyst or team of analysts they will follow. This includes some of the analysts at the big investment banks, who are regularly ranked by the likes of FX Week or Thomson Extel.

- Spread betting companies also offer their customers free seminars. These can be live and in person, or via a webinar. They continue to invest money in making sure new customers are being properly educated, but in addition they host some fairly advanced trading seminars as well. The best thing is: they're *free*. If you're a customer and can get to one, it is worth going along as you can also meet other traders and compare notes.

Data

Much of the data you will need is already available on your spread betting platform. However, some traders like to use additional data sources to support their trading activities. Much will depend on your budget, and how much you would like to spend. Here are some of the leading data providers for independent traders and investors:

ADVFN – www.advfn.com

You can easily lose yourself in ADVFN's amazing data archive. This is one of the most respected sites if you're considering spread betting shares. It has the advantage of allowing you to view Level 2 data. This shows you the size of trades being placed in the physical market, as well as the price they are being executed at. You are not viewing trading activity with your spread betting company, but it can show you how big trades are moving the price. ADVFN also offers coverage of forex and derivatives markets, and includes stock screening tools as part of its package. It remains highly rated by regular spread bettors.

Vectorvest – www.vectorvest.com

This is a US-based company, but it boasts data on over 18,000 shares globally. It seems perfectly adequate for tracking and analysing UK shares. Vectorvest, like ADVFN, has various different packages, going up in price depending on the level of information you are seeking.

Stockcharts – www.stockcharts.com

This is a massive resource for charting. Not only does it offer free and highly sophisticated charting for private traders, it also includes reams of analysis on developing charts. It also has a Chart School which lets you learn about technical analysis in your own time, if you don't have the time or the inclination to go to a seminar.

Magazines and newspapers

Financial Times – www.ft.com

I tend to make use of the FT's website rather than the newspaper, because it now boasts a great markets section, with many blogs from experienced FT journalists and other commentators. The FT is a great way to start the day, and I usually like to catch up on overnight news first thing in the morning. Regular features like 'The short view' are useful for helping to build an idea of the big picture and what the market is thinking. FT.com is also a useful research tool if you are looking back over a company's history, for example.

Investors Chronicle – www.investorschronicle.co.uk

The *Investors Chronicle* comes out every week and is one of the oldest and most respected stock market magazines in Europe. Its coverage is primarily the UK equities and funds market, and it has a strong personal finance slant. It is still fairly expensive, at over £100 per year, but if you are most interested in spread betting UK stocks, it may be worthwhile as a source of ideas, particularly for smaller companies.

Shares – www.sharesmagazine.com

Shares was set up by one of my old bosses at FT Business. Like the *Investors Chronicle*, it provides wide-ranging and comprehensive coverage of UK and European share markets, and in recent years, as the spread betting boom has continued, has expanded its coverage into other markets, like commodities and forex.

Moneyweek – www.moneyweek.com

The team at *Moneyweek* provide an excellent summary of what is going on in the world of business and money every week. Their coverage extends to non-equity asset classes, with regular articles on the commodities markets and forex. They also touch on spread betting on a frequent basis.

Your Trading Edge – www.ytemagazine.com

Your Trading Edge or *YTE* is an excellent bi-monthly magazine published in Australia. Although it does not cover spread betting specifically, and is aimed primarily at traders in Australia, it has broadened its coverage of global financial markets considerably. It is highly technical in nature, so if you favour charting, you will like it. Australian traders also tend to be fairly knowledgeable about commodities, hence there is plenty of discussion on global commodities markets. If anything can get you spread betting the ASX 200 or the Australian dollar, *YTE* will.

Websites

Twitter – www.twitter.com

Twitter is increasingly being used by traders as a source of breaking news. This is partly because many journalists and analysts now 'tweet' on a regular basis – sometimes as often as every 30 minutes when the market is open – and partly because it allows you, the trader, to build your own news feed by following the tweeters that interest you.

I've been particularly impressed over the past 18 months by the level of knowledge demonstrated by some of the active tweeters on the market. You can now use software that will help you to collate and monitor your favourite tweeters. By doing this, you are able to build up your own, comprehensive, tailored newsfeed. And it's all free!

YouTube – www.youtube.com

YouTube is a mine of information on trading, including spread betting. There are new videos being uploaded all the time. It is a reservoir of useful educational material for all levels of trading expertise. Many analysts also use it to broadcast daily commentary.

The Armchair Trader – www.thearmchairtrader.com

The Armchair Trader has been launched to provide information on margins and spreads for both the spread betting and CFD trading fraternity. It aims to offer an up-to-date picture of the various accounts on the market, and the spreads being offered on the most popular markets. In addition, it has news and articles on spread betting and CFD trading.

Digital Look – www.digitallook.com

Digital Look is an online news site with a strong focus on UK and European share markets. Its team of journalists are former newspaper and magazine writers. Apart from regular market updates, it also offers readers a large archive of company data, including corporate actions. DL is more to the tastes of the specialist share trader, but it does cover other markets like commodities and FX on occasion.

Television

CNBC and Bloomberg Television are both available via cable networks in Britain and are excellent sources of information on global markets. After lunchtime, their bias tends towards the US markets, with regular updates from the European news teams. If you have a tendency to be up in the middle of the night, you can also get a blow-by-blow account of what Asian markets are up to.

Both channels also offer solid coverage of the currency and commodities markets. I followed them closely during the 2008 financial crisis, and when working for CMC Markets, where television screens were strategically positioned at every corner of the dealing floor.

Some traders like having the television on in the background all day long, others don't. It can be possible to be caught up in the hysteria of what is going on if you listen too closely, and that can interfere with your discipline.

Trading coaches

There is a big business in advising and coaching traders, both professional and amateur. Many successful traders also have a lucrative side-line in training and advising other traders. Some spread bettors like to have someone on the end of the phone they can talk to when they are consistently losing money, who can advise them on where they might be going wrong.

Trading coaches are there to advise on strategy and technique. Some are only a step away from being psychiatrists. They are not investment advisers. They can't tell you whether a trade is a good one or not. They are most useful as an extra pair of eyes, looking over your shoulder – metaphorically or literally – and telling you where you're going wrong.

Spread betting can be a very solitary existence, and having someone else you can talk to objectively about your trading can be very helpful indeed in keeping your mind in the right place, and helping you to build a winning strategy.

Trading coaches don't come cheap: many of them are consulted by some of the best traders in the City, and some are very experienced in their own right. Retaining one can be expensive, but then again, like a good accountant, they can often save you more money than you pay them.

Trading coaches are best consulted when you are in the doldrums, and are taking some fairly consistent losses. It may just be the market, but it may have something to do with the way you are spread betting. UK-based coaches are probably a better choice if you are spread betting, as they will understand spread betting accounts and what the various providers are offering. There are some very good US coaches out there too, but they're further away, won't get up until lunchtime, and will be less familiar with UK and European markets.

When choosing a trading coach, make sure they are someone who knows what they're doing, and has a track record in trading and advising successful trading. Word of mouth from other traders is often as good a means as any of finding the right one for you. But be prepared to pay for good advice.

Systematic trading programs

There is now a large industry in the US selling software packages that help you to trade by generating buy and sell signals. These are sometimes described as 'black box' trading strategies or trading 'robots'. Over the years, many traders and programmers have designed their own systems for trading, and some of these are now becoming commercially available as software packages.

In the world of hedge funds and investment banking, computer programs are being widely used because computers enjoy a number of advantages over human traders:

1 Computers don't get emotional about losing trades.

2 Computers learn more quickly from their mistakes.

3 Computers can process far more market information, more accurately, than humans.

4 At the institutional level, computers can trade more quickly than humans, and react to price changes in the market more effectively.

Using a computer program to trade for yourself is a hit-and-miss affair. A program will need to be one suited to the particular market you want to trade, and the risk parameters you want to use. Using a program that was designed to trade shares to bet on forex markets can go badly awry. You will also frequently need to provide it with the historical data it requires to make its calculations, as well as make sure it is hooked up to a current data feed. This in itself can be expensive – live data feeds do not come cheap!

The new generation of trading programs coming onto the market are more flexible, and allow you to tailor them a little to your own requirements. You are still drawing on the core algorithm for your principal trading signals, but you can adjust it to suit your own personal objectives and risk tolerance.

Computer-based trading programs are something of a leap of faith if you have not designed them yourself. Having said that, they must be doing something right, because some spread betting companies have been known to close the accounts of traders who they suspect are using a program-based approach.

Designing your own program to trade can be challenging, unless you are something of a software engineer yourself. It is not a fire-and-forget process: programs need to be constantly updated and tweaked. In addition, they rely heavily on past performance data to inform their trading decisions. What they don't tend to take into consideration is that markets are always changing, they are never static, and this makes them unpredictable.

Having said that, an estimated 30–40 per cent of London share market volume on a daily basis is being handled by algorithmic trading strategies these days. The machines are playing a bigger and bigger role in financial markets.

Reading list

There is a wide and comprehensive range of books available on trading and spread betting, many written by industry insiders or those with professional trading experience. Below are some of those which might help the newcomer with additional insights on the markets and spread betting in general. Much really depends on which areas of the wide world of financial markets you wish to focus on, and how your trading strategy evolves.

Spread betting

Burns, Robbie (2010) *The Naked Trader's Guide To Spread Betting*, London: Harriman House

Jones, David (2010) *Spread Betting the Forex Market*, London: Harriman House

Pryor, Malcolm (2007) *The Financial Spread Betting Handbook*, London: Harriman House

Trading

Faith, Curtis M. (2007) *Way of the Turtle*, New York: McGraw-Hill

Laidi, Ashraf (2008) *Currency Trading & Intermarket Analysis*, London: John Wiley & Sons

Schwager, Jack (1992) *The New Market Wizards*, New York: Collins Business

Tharp, Van K. (1998) *Trade Your Way to Financial Freedom*, New York: McGraw-Hill

Technical analysis

Gifford, Elli (1995) *Technical Analysis – Predicting Price Action in the Market*, London: FT Pitman Publishing

Nison, Steve (2001) *Japanese Candlestick Charting Techniques: A contemporary guide to the ancient investment techniques of the Far East*, 2nd edn, Upper Saddle River, NJ: Prentice Hall

Glossary of spread betting and other financial market terms

ADX (average directional index) A popular type of technical analysis, used to measure the strength of a trend. On its own it does not indicate whether this is an up or down trend, but an ADX of 20–30 can represent the beginning of a trend. It is often used in conjunction with other data by trend followers.

Aussie Slang term used by currency traders for the Australian dollar.

Bear market A market following a consistent downward trend.

Bid price Also known as the 'buy' price. The price used to open a long bet, or to close a short bet.

Bid-to-cover ratio A term used to measure demand for a particular investment being sold at auction. This is often used to assess demand for government debt, for example. A ratio of over 2.0 equates to a fairly aggressive auction with plenty of demand for that security. The ratio is calculated by either dividing the number of bids received by the number of bids accepted, or the value of bids received divided by the value of bids accepted.

Bid/offer spread The difference between the buy and the sell price, and one of the ways spread betting companies make their money. Also, wider spreads reflect markets where there is less liquidity.

Binary bet A type of spread bet where you win or lose depending on whether a market price crosses a specific level. Traders either collect 100 per cent of their winnings or get nothing.

Bollinger band A technical analysis term for two lines plotted above and below the moving average. They are meant to help to measure the relative volatility of the market concerned.

Bonds Debt securities which usually pay out a regular rate of interest to their owner. Bonds can be issued by governments, municipalities, companies and some other entities.

Breakout A breakout occurs when a range-bound market suddenly moves outside an established trading range. It is keenly sought by short-term traders and technical analysts.

Brent Crude The benchmark oil futures contract for non-US oil.

Bull market A market which is moving in a consistently upwards direction.

Cable A term frequently used to describe the GBP/USD currency market.

CFD (contract for difference) A popular over-the-counter trading instrument that is now one of the most widely traded retail derivatives outside the UK and Ireland. Unlike spread bets, however, CFDs do incur tax. They are often used for FX trading.

Counterparty The other party on the other side of your trade or investment. It takes two to tango with any financial transaction. In the case of spread betting, this will be your spread betting company, but in turn your spread betting company will have credit lines with banks, as well as open trades with prime brokers.

Coupon Term sometimes used to describe the rate of interest paid out on a bond. This harks back to the days when bond issuers printed a paper certificate with coupons on it that could be redeemed for interest payments.

Demo account A trial account offered by many spread betting companies which you can open with no money. Usually you will only be able to spread bet on a restricted list of markets, and often you will only have access to the platform for a limited period of time – two weeks is typical. The intention is to give you a feel for the functionality of the platform, as well as to allow you to trade – and potentially make mistakes – without risking any real money.

Direct market access (DMA) The process of trading directly on the market, or at the very least being able to see individual orders coming into the market, and being able to act on them.

Deposit requirement The amount of money a spread betting company requires the trader to have on deposit in order to place a bet in a given market. This will vary from company to company.

Eurodollar The market for lending and borrowing US dollars outside the United States banking system.

Fibonacci numbers A mathematical term for numbers which are part of a Fibonacci sequence. A Fibonacci sequence is a series of numbers created by adding the two previous numbers in the sequence: for example 0, 1, 1, 2, 3, 5, 8, 13, 21, 34, 55, etc.

Fibonacci retracements A form of technical analysis used to try and predict how far a market will turn against a trend before resuming its original direction. It is created by taking two extreme points on a chart, and dividing the vertical distance by the key Fibonacci ratios – e.g 23.6 per cent, 38.2 per cent, 50 per cent, 61.8 per cent and 100 per cent. All these ratios are based on the relationships between numbers in the Fibonacci sequence.

Head and shoulders A favoured technical pattern that is defined by two successively higher peaks in the market price, followed by a lower peak. This is often seen by analysts as the top of the market, and evidence that it is beginning to lose momentum.

Greenback Slang term used to describe the US dollar.

If done A type of spread betting order that takes place if a previous order is executed. For example, this can be used to place a stop loss at the same time another order is opened. Some traders use 'if done' orders if they cannot be at the screens all the time, and need to take advantage of potential price levels.

Japanese candlestick A form of technical analysis pioneered by sixteenth-century Japanese rice traders. It shows not only the highest and lowest points reached by a market over a given time frame, but also the opening and closing price at either end of the time frame. Candlesticks can be defined by the user to cover any regular time period they care to analyse.

JGB (Japanese government bond) Debt issued by the Japanese government. The benchmark price of Japan's sovereign debt is the 10 year JGB.

Leverage A term commonly used to describe the act of borrowing money with which to invest.

LIBOR London Interbank Offered Rate, the daily rate used by banks to borrow from each other in the London money markets. This is frequently used as a benchmark rate for financial products.

Liquidity A term used to describe how easy it is to buy and sell in a market. A less liquid market can make it harder for someone to buy or sell large quantities of an asset. If markets become less liquid, spreads tend to get wider.

Limit order An automatic instruction to the broker to close your bet once a specific price level is reached.

Loonie Slang term used by currency traders to describe the Canadian dollar.

Margin The minimum amount of money you need to commit to open a spread bet. Your spread betting company should allow you to deposit more than this if you need to.

Margin call If you are close to losing your margin amount, your broker may call you up to ask you to deposit more money in the trade. For example, if you staked £100, you might get a call when you had lost £80. Brokers will make margin calls on a discretionary basis.

Moving average A line on a chart generated by using the average price performance over a specific period of previous days. By keeping tabs on the moving average, traders can see how the current market behaviour compares to past performance. Typical moving average series include 200, 50 and 30 day periods.

NTR (Notional trading requirement) A measurement used by spread betting companies to determine whether you have enough money in your account to fund a trade. This goes beyond stumping up the initial margin. Each market has a different bet size requirement which the company will apply to your cash balance to determine whether you can afford the bet if the market turns against you.

OCO (one cancels the other) A type of spread betting order which will instruct the platform to cancel a second order if a primary order is executed. For example, if an automatic take profit order occurs, the trader will also want to make sure that the stop loss protecting the trade has also been cancelled. This is an automated order which can be added to ensure that something happens even when you are away from your trading screen.

OTC (over the counter) A trade that is not taking place in an open exchange. Most liquid futures markets are now based on one of the big derivatives exchanges, but not all of them.

Offer price Also known as the sell price, this is the price used to go short of a market, or to close a long bet.

Pairs trading The practice of exploiting the difference between two prices – usually shares – that move in tandem. If they are seen to be beginning to move apart, spread bettors can use simultaneous long and short bets to try to make money off the expectation that they will eventually revert to normal behaviour. This strategy is often employed using the shares of two companies that compete in the same line of business.

Pip A term used in foreign exchange trading circles to mean the digit furthest to the right on any forex quote. A currency is described as moving a certain number of 'pips'. If, for example, yen dropped from 84.62 against the US dollar to 84.51, it would have dropped 11 pips.

Point A single 'unit' of the market you are spread betting. This will vary from market to market. Many stock market indexes are quoted in points already. This is also the number you are betting on. It is usually the number on the far right of any market quote.

Quantitative easing The process by which a central bank buys financial assets like bonds in order to inject more money into the financial system. It does not actually print new physical bank notes, but it does create the money it uses to acquire the assets.

Range-bound A range-bound market is one that moves between two price points, an upper and a lower one. The market lacks any real momentum, and the price tends not to break out of the trading range.

RBOB Literally, 'reformulated blendstock for oxygen blending', this is the commonly traded US gasoline or refined petroleum futures contract. You will often see it quoted on spread betting platforms simply as 'RBOB'.

Resistance level A point above which a market tends not to rise: too many traders are selling at that price, forcing it back down again. This can contribute to a range-bound market if there is also a support level in play (see below).

Rollover The process of automatically renewing a bet overnight or when it reaches its expiry date. This usually incurs a financing charge from the spread betting company.

RSI (relative strength index) An indicator used to demonstrate whether a market is being overbought or oversold, using historical prices as a reference. Usually, an RSI of more than 70 indicates an overbought market, and one under 30 an oversold one.

Shares Securities issued by a company which confer a share in the ownership of that company. These can be freely traded on the stock market. Profits in the company can be paid back to shareholders in the form of dividends.

Short When you go short on a market, you are in a position to make money if the market is going down in value.

Short sterling A spread bet that allows the trader to take advantage of changes in UK base rates. Its price is based on future interest rate expectations, and is calculated by subtracting the expected rate from 100.

Softs The market for agricultural commodities, namely products that are not energy or metals-based commodities.

Spot price The price for settlement of a particular future were it to be settled today. Sometimes this is calculated using sophisticated mathematical estimates. It is not always possible to trade on the spot price, but it is becoming increasingly common in spread betting circles.

Stocks Another term for shares (see above).

Stop loss An automatic order to your broker to close your position at a loss if it reaches a specified price. It is used to protect spread bettors from major losses.

Support level A price below which a given market tends not to drop, usually because it becomes cheap enough for some buyers to enter the market. If this happens consistently enough, analysts can see it as a support level. Technical analysis can also sometimes be used to predict where a support level will be.

Swing trading The practice of repeatedly trading the same market both short and long while it is trading between two ranges. The swing trader actively exploits price drops as well as price rises.

Tick Term used to describe the minimum price unit by which a market can change. In spread betting, this will be the 'points' you stake money against. Also called 'pips' in forex parlance.

Tick rate The minimum price move of a particular spread bet.

Toppy Analysts describe a market as 'toppy' if they think it has become over-priced and is likely to correct (i.e. drop in price).

Trailing stop loss A type of stop loss that trails dynamically behind the trade. You need to decide how far behind it follows. If the market then falls back, it closes the trade. This allows you to lock in profits from a trade even when you are away from your trading screen. Not all spread betting companies offer trailing stop losses, but they are becoming increasingly popular.

Trigger line An indicator used in charts where MACD (Moving Average Convergence Divergence) is being monitored. If the MACD crosses the trigger line, it can be a signal to buy or sell, depending on the direction the MACD is heading. A downwards cross can indicate a market entering a bear phase.

Troy ounce Standard measurement of gold. The gold price is typically quoted in dollars per troy ounce. It is slightly over 31 grams in actual weight.

VIX An index used to measure volatility in the S&P 500 index, often referred to as the Fear Index. It is sometimes made available as a spread bet. It tends to rise during periods of market uncertainty.

WTI West Texas Intermediate – the benchmark crude oil contract for North America.

Appendix: Major spread betting providers

Name	Website	Minimum account (£)	Demo platform	Education	Phone	Mobile trading	Short description
Accendo Markets	www.accendomarkets.com	0	Y	Y	0203 051 7461	Y	Founded in 2008, Accendo Markets platform and back end systems are powered by IG Index. Formerly an advisory CFD broker, it now places considerable emphasis on personal service, including phone dealing.
Capital Spreads	www.capitalspreads.com	0	Y	Y	0207 456 7020	Y	A trading name of London Capital Group which was founded in 1996, Capital Spreads was launched in 2003.
City Index	www.cityindex.co.uk	100	N	Y	0845 355 0801	Y	Established in 1983, City Index provides spread betting, CFD and FX trading services globally. As part of the privately owned IPGL, City Index acquired the IFX Group in 2005 and now owns spread betting business, Finspreads.com.
CMC Markets	www.cmcmarkets.co.uk	0	Y	Online	0207 170 8200	Y	Founded in 1989 by Peter Cruddas as a Foreign Exchange market maker, CMC Markets launched its spread betting service under the name deal4free in 2001. The business now has a large international presence with key markets in the UK, Europe and Australia.
ETX Capital	www.etxcapital.co.uk	100	N	Y	0800 138 4582	Y	ETX Capital is the trading name of Monecor (London) Limited which was established in 1965. Originally part of Tradition Bank under the name TradIndex, ETX Capital was launched in 2007.
GFT UK	www.gftuk.com	0	Y	Y	0800 358 0864	Y	Founded in 1997 as a US Forex business, GFT launched its UK spread betting business in 2006.
IG Index	www.igindex.co.uk	0	N	Y	0800 195 3100	Y	Founded by Stuart Wheeler in 1974, IG Index is listed on the London Stock Exchange as a constituent of the FTSE 250.
MF Global Markets	www.mfglobalmarkets.com	0	Y	Online	0203 321 5678	N	Formerly Man Financial, MF Global is a global derivatives broker that can trace its roots back to the sugar trading business back in 1783.
Saxo Bank	www.saxospreads.com	0	Y	Online	0207 456 7075	N	Saxo Bank Financial Spreads is a trading name of London Capital Group Holdings plc. Established in 1992, Saxo Banks headquarters are based in Copenhagen, Denmark.
Worldspreads	www.worldspreads.com	100	N	Online / Seminars	0800 987 5800	N	Founded in 2000, Worldspreads head office is in London. The business is listed on the Alternative Investment Market and is regulated by the FSA.

Index

Comprehensive. Authoritative. Trusted

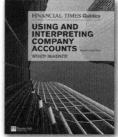

9780273723967

9780273727873

9780273723745

9780273745822

9780273722014

9780273729846

9780273712671

9780273724520

9780273729105

9780273727835

9780273763031

9780273729969

9780273736868

9780273761990

9780273756668

FINANCIAL TIMES Guides
INVESTING FOR INCOME
GROW YOUR INCOME THROUGH SMARTER INVESTING
DAVID STEVENSON

FINANCIAL TIMES Guides
STRATEGY
HOW TO CREATE AND DELIVER A WINNING STRATEGY
FOURTH EDITION
RICHARD KOCH

FINANCIAL TIMES Guides
UNDERSTANDING FINANCE
A NO-NONSENSE COMPANION TO FINANCIAL TOOLS AND TECHNIQUES
JAVIER ESTRADA

9780273735656   9780273745471   9780273738022

FINANCIAL TIMES Guides
WEALTH MANAGEMENT
HOW TO PLAN, PROTECT AND INVEST YOUR ASSETS
JASON BUTLER

FINANCIAL TIMES Guides
BUSINESS COACHING
ANNE SCOULAR

FINANCIAL TIMES Guides
FINANCE FOR NON-FINANCIAL MANAGERS
JO HAIGH

FINANCIAL TIMES Guides
FINANCIAL SPREAD BETTING
STUART FIELDHOUSE

9780273742999   9780273734444   9780273756200   9780273750468

FINANCIAL TIMES Guides
HOW THE STOCK MARKET REALLY WORKS
FIFTH EDITION
LEO GOUGH

FINANCIAL TIMES Guides
FINANCIAL MARKETS
GLEN ARNOLD

FINANCIAL TIMES Guides
TECHNICAL ANALYSIS
HOW TO TRADE LIKE A PROFESSIONAL
JACINTA CHAN

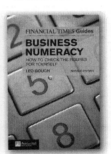

FINANCIAL TIMES Guides
BUSINESS NUMERACY
HOW TO CHECK THE FIGURES FOR YOURSELF
LEO GOUGH

9780273743552   9780273730002   9780273751335   9780273746430

Change your business life today